CAMBRIDGE PRIMARY Mathematics

Challenge

Name: _____

Contents

Addition and subtraction (1) 4–5

Length 6–7

Tens and ones 8–9

Estimating 10–11

2D and 3D shapes and symmetry 12–14

Two-digit numbers (counting beyond 20) 15–17

Capacity and weight 18–19

Telling the time 20–21

Odd and even numbers 22–23

Ordinal numbers and ordering 24–25

Addition and subtraction (2) 26–29

Patterns 30–31

Money 32

Length, capacity and time 33–35

Sorting and representing data (1) 36–37

Adding and subtracting tens and ones 38–39

Equivalence 40–41

Doubles and halves 42–43

Addition and subtraction (3) 44–45

Money, length, capacity and time 46–49

Sorting and representing data (2) 50–51

Photocopiable resources 52–60

Answers 61–64

Cherri Moseley and Janet Rees

CAMBRIDGE UNIVERSITY PRESS

CAMBRIDGE
UNIVERSITY PRESS

University Printing House, Cambridge CB2 8BS, United Kingdom
One Liberty Plaza, 20th Floor, New York, NY 10006, USA
477 Williamstown Road, Port Melbourne, VIC 3207, Australia
4843/24, 2nd Floor, Ansari Road, Daryaganj, Delhi – 110002, India
79 Anson Road, #06–04/06, Singapore 079906

Cambridge University Press is part of the University of Cambridge.

It furthers the University's mission by disseminating knowledge in the pursuit of education, learning and research at the highest international levels of excellence.

www.cambridge.org
Information on this title: education.cambridge.org/9781316509197

© Cambridge University Press 2016

This publication is in copyright. Subject to statutory exception and to the provisions of relevant collective licensing agreements, no reproduction of any part may take place without the written permission of Cambridge University Press.

First published 2016
20 19 18 17 16 15 14 13 12 11 10 9 8 7 6

Printed in Spain by GraphyCems

A catalogue record for this publication is available from the British Library

ISBN 978-1-316-50919-7 Paperback

Cambridge University Press has no responsibility for the persistence or accuracy of URLs for external or third-party internet websites referred to in this publication, and does not guarantee that any content on such websites is, or will remain, accurate or appropriate.

NOTICE TO TEACHERS
It is illegal to reproduce any part of this work in material form (including photocopying and electronic storage) except under the following circumstances:
(i) where you are abiding by a licence granted to your school or institution by the Copyright Licensing Agency;
(ii) where no such licence exists, or where you wish to exceed the terms of a license, and you have gained the written permission of Cambridge University Press;
(iii) where you are allowed to reproduce without permission under the provisions of Chapter 3 of the Copyright, Designs and Patents Act 1988, which covers, for example, the reproduction of short passages within certain types of educational anthology and reproduction for the purposes of setting examination questions.

NOTICE TO TEACHERS IN THE UK
The photocopy masters in this publication may be photocopied or distributed (electronically) free of charge for classroom use within the school or institution that purchased the publication. Worksheets and copies of them remain in the copyright of Cambridge University Press, and such copies may not be distributed or used in any way outside the purchasing institution.

This book is part of the Cambridge Primary Maths project. This is an innovative combination of curriculum and resources designed to support teachers and learners to succeed in primary mathematics through best-practice international maths teaching and a problem-solving approach.

To get involved, visit
www.cie.org.uk/cambridgeprimarymaths.

Introduction

This ***Challenge activity book*** is part of a series of 12 write-in activity books for primary mathematics grades 1–6. It can be used as a standalone book, but the content also complements *Cambridge Primary Maths*. Learners progress at different rates, so this series provides a Challenge and Skills Builder activity book for each Primary Mathematics Curriculum Framework Stage to broaden the depth of and to support further learning.

The *Challenge* books extend learning by providing stretching activities to increase the depth of maths knowledge and skills. Support is given through short reminders of key information, topic vocabulary, and hints to prompt learning. These books have been written to support learners whose first language is not English.

How to use the books

The activities are for use by learners in school or at home, with adult mediation. Topics have been carefully chosen to focus on those areas where learners can stretch their depth of knowledge. The approach is linked directly to *Cambridge Primary Maths*, but teachers and parents can pick and choose which activities to cover, or go through the books in sequence.

The varied set of activities grow in challenge through each unit, including:

- closed questions with answers, so progress can be checked
- questions with more than one possible answer
- activities requiring resources, for example, dice, spinners or digit cards
- activities and games best done with someone else, in class or at home, which give the opportunity for parents and teachers to be fully involved in the child's learning
- activities to support different learning styles: working individually, in pairs, in groups.

How to approach the activities

Space is provided for learners to write their answers in the book. Some activities might need further practice or writing, so students could be given a blank notebook at the start of the year to use alongside the book. Each activity follows a standard structure.

- **Remember** gives an overview of key learning points. It introduces core concepts and, later, can be used as a revision guide. These sections should be read with an adult who can check understanding before attempting the activities.
- **Vocabulary** assists with difficult mathematical terms, particularly when English is not the learner's first language. Learners should read through the key vocabulary with an adult and be encouraged to clarify understanding.
- **Hints** prompt and assist in building understanding, and steer the learner in the right direction.
- **You will need** gives teachers and parents a list of resources for each activity.
- **Photocopiable resources** are provided at the end of the book, for easy assembly in class or at home.
- **Links** to the Cambridge International Examinations Primary Mathematics Curriculum Framework objectives and the corresponding *Cambridge Primary Mathematics Teacher's Resource* are given in the footnote on every page.
- **Calculators** should be used to help learners understand numbers and the number system, including place value and properties of numbers. However, the calculator is not promoted as a calculation tool before Stage 5.

Note:

When a 'spinner' is included, put a paperclip flat on the page so the end is over the centre of the spinner. Place the pencil point in the centre of the spinner, through the paperclip. Hold the pencil firmly and spin the paperclip to generate a result.

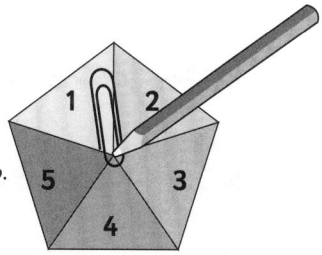

Tracking progress

Answers to closed questions are given at the back of the book – these allow teachers, parents and learners to check their work.

When completing each activity, teachers and parents are advised to encourage self-assessment by asking the students how straightforward they found the activity. When learners are reflecting on games, they should consider how challenging the mathematics was, not who won. Learners could use a ✓/✗ or red/green colouring system to record their self-assessment anywhere on each activity page.

These assessments provide teachers and parents with an understanding of how best to support individual learners' next steps.

Caterpillar numbers

Remember
When you are counting forwards or backwards, the numbers are always in the same order.

Vocabulary
0, 1, 2, 3, 4, 5, 6, 7, 8, 9, 10, 11, 12, number, number pair, number bond, double, count on, add, equals

Solve each clue.
Cross off the answer on the caterpillar.
The number that is left is the secret number.

It is not 2 + 3.

It is not 0 + 1.

It is not 4 + 5.

It is not 7 + 3.

It is not 2 + 0.

It is not 4 + 2.

It is not 0 + 0.

It is not 2 + 2.

It is not 6 + 2.

It is not 1 + 2.

The secret number is ☐

Hint: Use the number track to support counting on.

0	1	2	3	4	5	6	7	8	9	10	11	12

Unit 1A Number and problem solving
CPM Framework 1Nn1, 1Nn2, 1Nc1, 1Nc2, 1Nc8, 1Nc11, 1Pt1, 1Pt2; CPM Teacher's Resource 1A: 2.1, 2.3, 4.1

Aeroplane numbers

Vocabulary
0, 1, 2, 3, 4, 5, 6, 7, 8, 9, 10, 11, 12, number, number pair, number bond, count on, count back, add, take away, equals

Solve each clue.
Cross off the answer on the aeroplane.
The number that is left is the secret number.

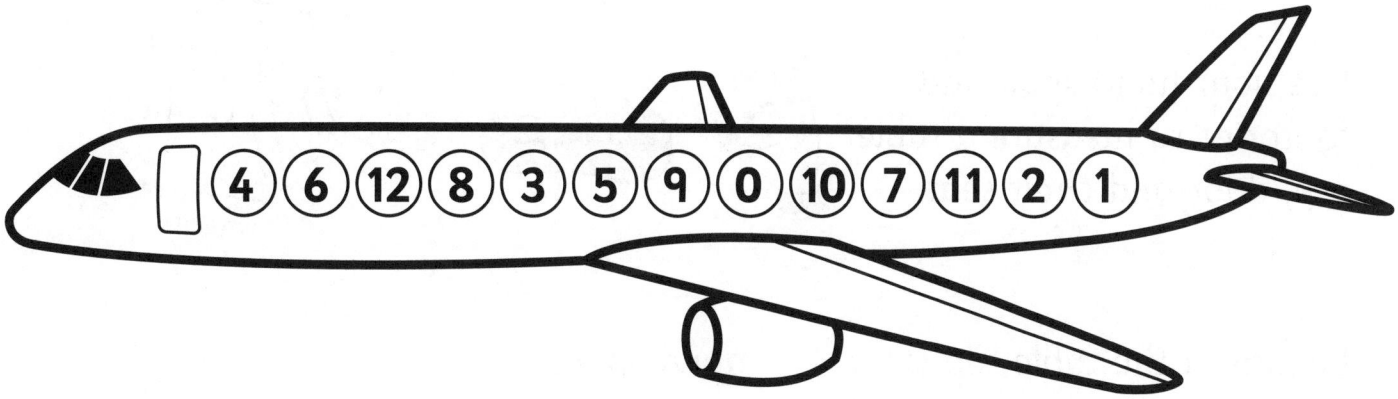

It is not 4 + 3.

It is not 7 – 7.

It is not 3 + 5.

It is not 9 – 8.

It is not 8 + 2.

It is not 9 – 7.

It is not 7 + 4.

It is not 11 – 5.

It is not 3 + 6.

It is not 10 – 5.

It is not 8 + 4.

It is not 11 – 7.

The secret number is ☐

Hint: Use the number track to support counting on or back.

0	1	2	3	4	5	6	7	8	9	10	11	12

Hands and feet

You will need: a cut-out of your own footprint

Remember
Do not leave any spaces when you measure.

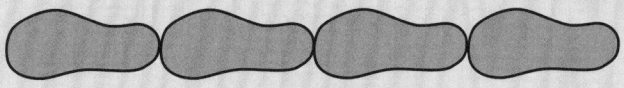

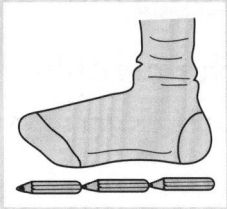

Vocabulary
measure, compare, about the same, roughly, length, width

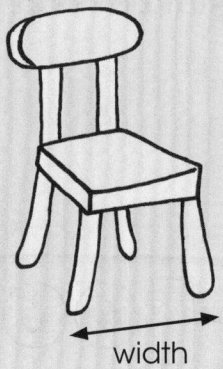

Use your hand span and footprint to measure a table top, door and chair seat.

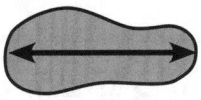

Length of the table top is ☐ hand spans.

Length of the table top is ☐ footprints.

Width of the door is ☐ hand spans.

Width of the door is ☐ footprints.

Width of the chair seat is ☐ hand spans.

Width of the chair seat is ☐ footprints.

Are the measures of each object the same? Explain why.

Hint: Keep the hand span the same width when measuring.

Snakes

Remember
Do not leave any spaces between the cubes.

You will need: a set of cubes all the same size, for example, 2 centimetre interlocking cubes

Vocabulary
measure, compare, long, short, longer, shorter, longest, shortest

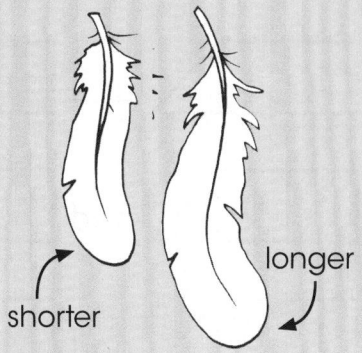

Use cubes to measure the length of each snake.

 ☐ cubes

 ☐ cubes

 ☐ cubes

 ☐ cubes

 ☐ cubes

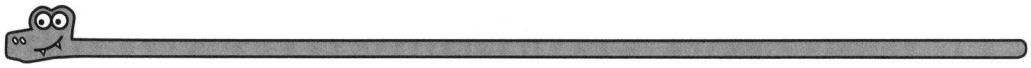 ☐ cubes

The longest snake is ☐ cubes long.

The shortest snake is ☐ cubes long.

Colour snakes that are shorter than your pencil green.

Colour snakes that are longer than your pencil red.

Tens and ones

Remember
Two-digit numbers are made from tens and ones.
For example, 18 is 1 ten and 8 ones, 10 and 8.

You will need:
place-value cards for 1, 2, 4, 6, 9 and 10, from resource 1, pages 52–3

Vocabulary
addition, total, digit, tens, ones, place-value cards, arrow cards, lowest, highest

Use the place-value cards to make numbers between 10 and 20.

1 0 and ☐ make ☐.

1 0 and ☐ make ☐.

1 0 and ☐ make ☐.

1 0 and ☐ make ☐.

1 0 and ☐ make ☐.

The lowest number I made is ☐.

The highest number I made is ☐.

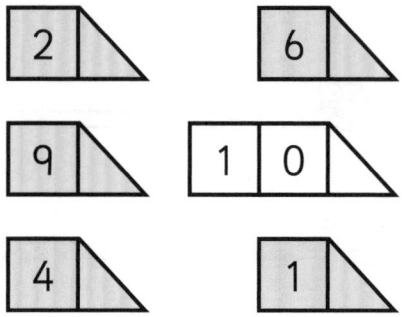

Some numbers between 10 and 20 cannot be made with these cards.
Write the numbers that cannot be made.

Hint: Count from 10 to 20 to find out which numbers are missing.

Numbers to 50

You will need:
resource 1, pages 52–3

Remember
The first digit in a two-digit number tells you how many tens, the second digit tells you how many ones.

1	2	3	4	5	6	7	8	9	10
11	12	13	14	15	16	17	18	19	20
21	22	23	24	25	26	27	28	29	30
31	32	33	34	35	36	37	38	39	40
41	42	43	44	45	46	47	48	49	50

Complete the place-value cards for each circled number.

12 is 1 0 and 2 .

31 is and .

19 is and .

37 is and .

23 is and .

45 is and .

26 is and .

48 is and .

Circle two more numbers. Complete the place-value cards for those numbers.

is and .

is and .

Hint: Use place-value cards to make each number.

My hand

Remember
An estimate does not have to be the right answer. It is a sensible guess. The more you practise estimating, the more accurate you will become.

You will need:
counters, cubes

Vocabulary
estimate, count

Hint: Put the counters or cubes into tens to help to count them.

Draw around your hand.

Estimate how many cubes will cover your hand picture.
Cover your hand picture with a single layer of cubes. Count the cubes.

My estimate ☐ cubes. My counted number ☐ cubes.

Estimate how many counters will cover your hand picture.
Cover your hand picture with a single layer of counters. Count them.

My estimate ☐ counters. My counted number ☐ counters.

Use the words **cubes** and **counters** to complete the sentence:

I needed more _____ than _____ to cover my hand.

Unit 1A Number and problem solving
CPM Framework 1Nn2, 1Nn3, 1Nn6, 1Nn8, 1Nn11, 1Pt2, 1Pt9; CPM Teacher's Resource 5.1, 5.2

Number line numbers

Remember
Numbers that are halfway between 2 tens numbers have 5 ones.

You will need:
resource 2, page 54

Estimate where each balloon should be joined to the number line.
Draw the string to each balloon from the correct place on the number line.

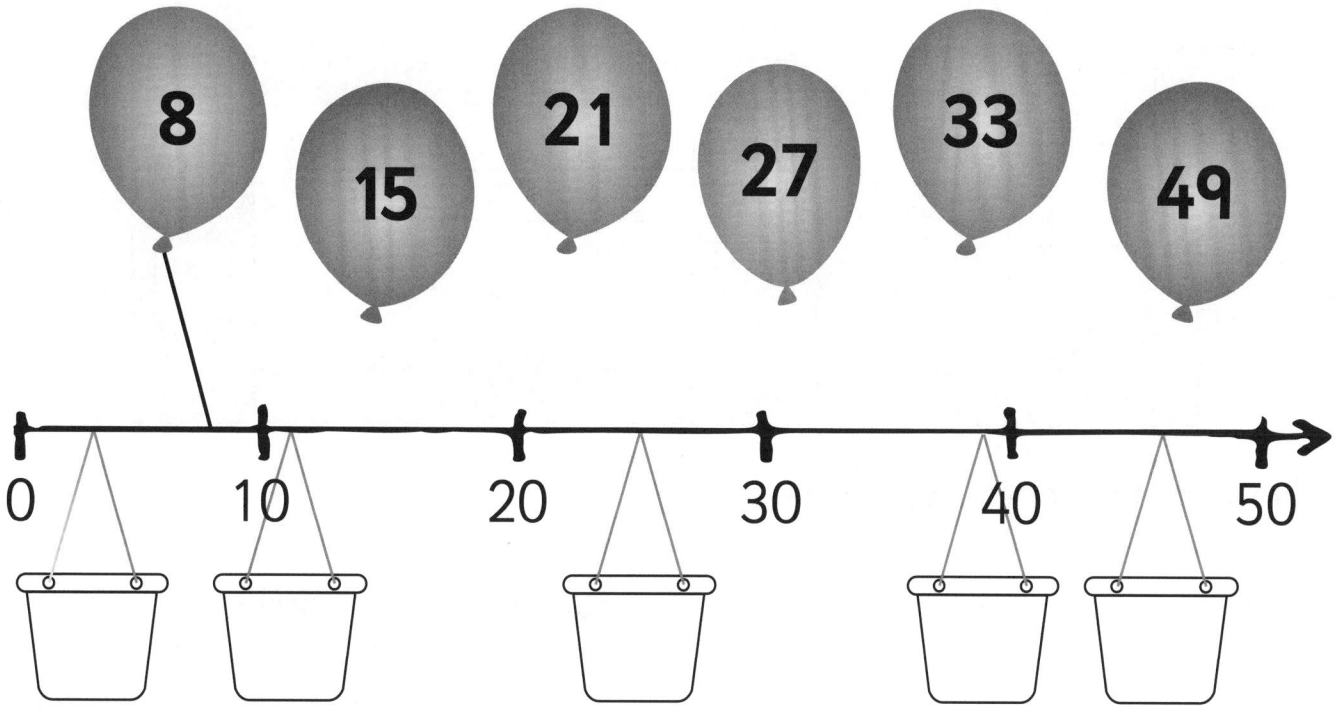

Estimate which number belongs in each basket.
Write the number in the basket.

Hint: Use the tens numbers to help.

2D shapes

Remember
2D shapes are flat.

Vocabulary

circle

square

rectangle

triangle

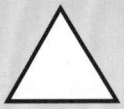

Look at the climbing frame.

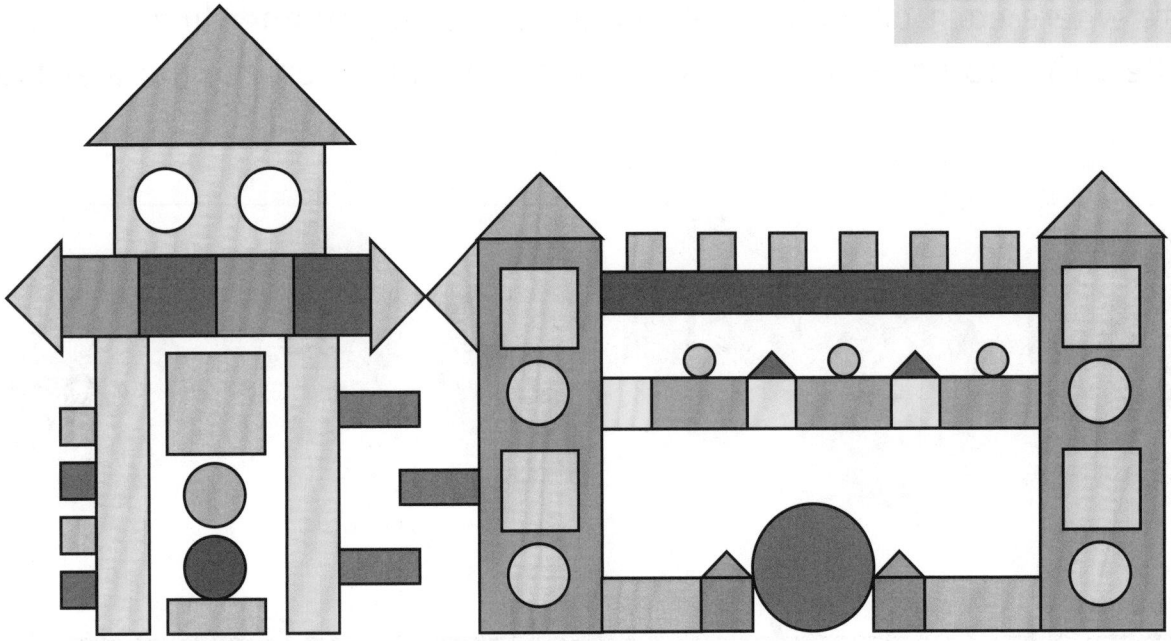

How many shapes can you see?

I can see ☐ triangles.

I can see ☐ circles.

I can see ☐ squares.

I can see ☐ rectangles.

Draw your own climbing frame with
4 circles, 2 triangles, 6 squares and 3 rectangles.

3D shapes

Remember
3D shapes are solid.

You will need:
everyday shapes

Vocabulary
corner, side, edge, face, 3D

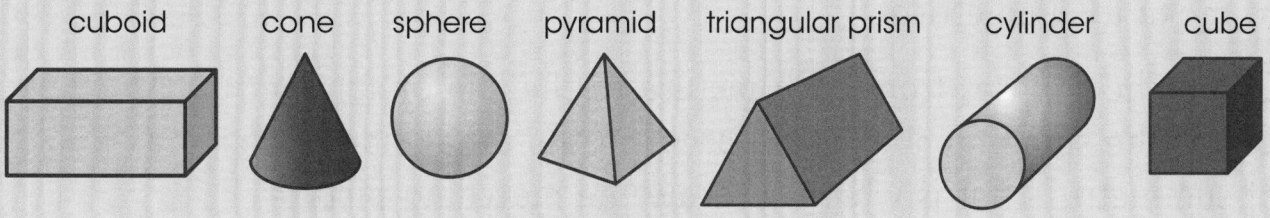

Look for 3D shapes that are in everyday objects.
Draw or write the name of the shape.

I have
6 flat faces.

All my faces are squares.

_____

I have
5 flat faces.

1 face is a square and 4 faces are triangles.

_____

Choose a 3D shape and write a set of clues for it.

_____

_____

_____

_____

_____

_____

_____

_____

I have 1 flat face and
1 curved surface.

My flat face is a circle.

_____

I have 2 flat faces and
1 curved surface.

My flat faces are circles.

_____

Symmetry

You will need: a mirror

Remember
In a symmetrical shape, each half is a mirror image of the other.

Vocabulary
symmetrical

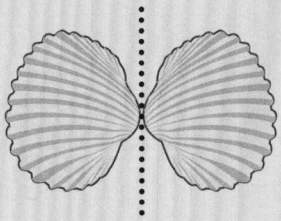

Add pictures to the right-hand side of the grid to make it symmetrical.

Count the squares from each picture to the line of symmetry. Count the same number of squares, on the other side of the line of symmetry. That is where to draw the matching picture.

line of symmetry

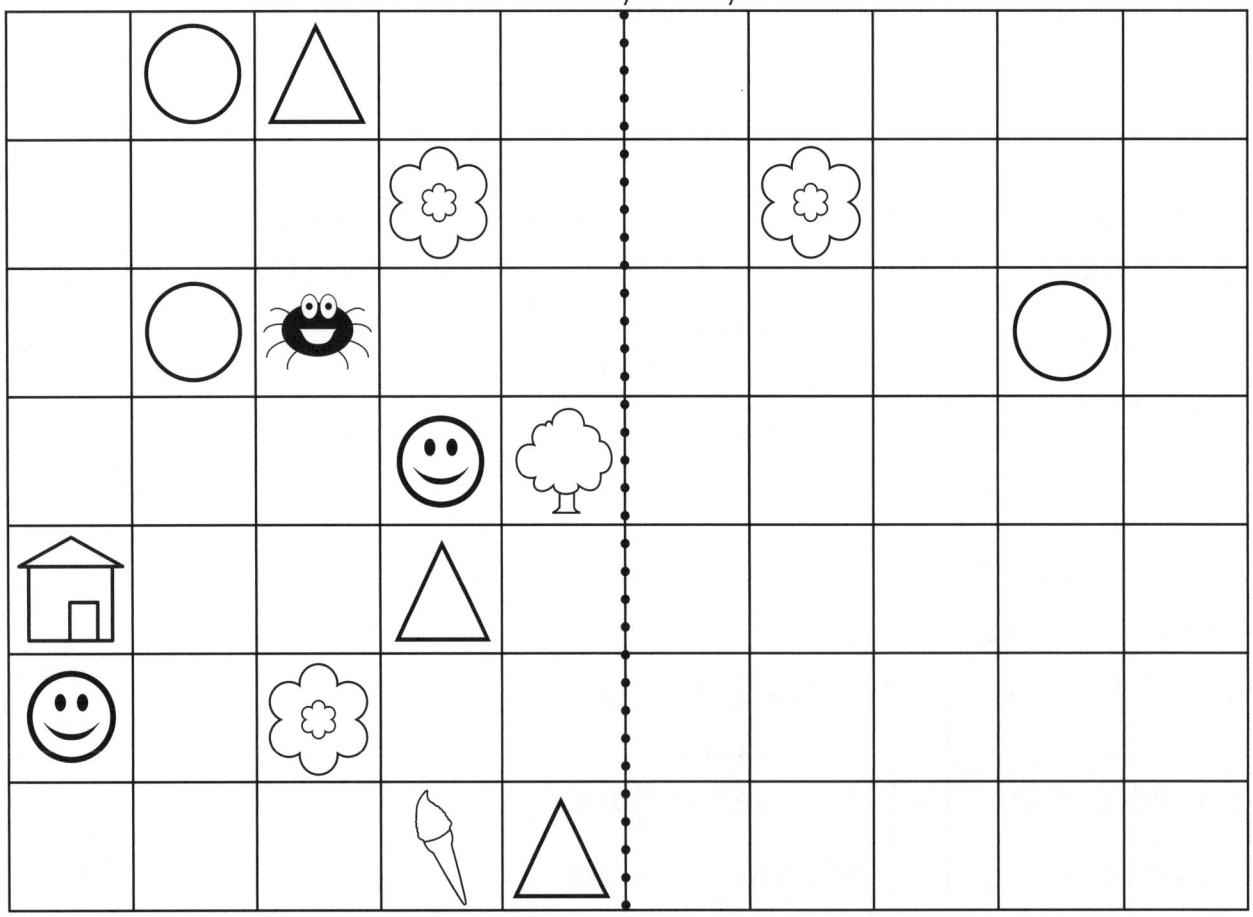

Hint: Put the mirror on the line of symmetry to check that the finished grid is symmetrical.

Number spinners

Remember
Two-digit numbers are made from tens and ones.

You will need: resource 1, pages 52–53, resource 2, page 54, a pencil and paperclip to use the spinners

Vocabulary
number pair, addition, total, digit, place-value cards, arrow cards, 100 square

Spin both spinners to make a two-digit number.
Write the numbers on the place-value cards.

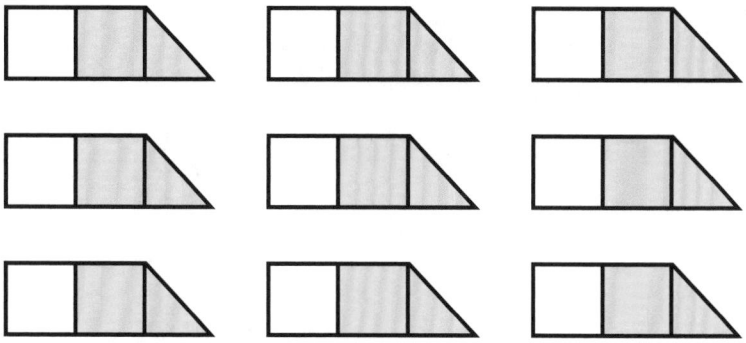

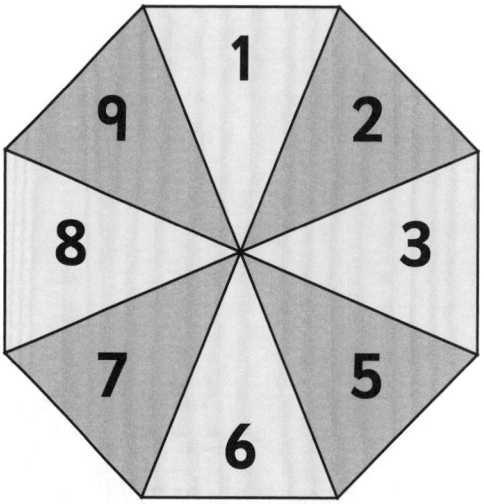

Which two-digit numbers cannot be made?
Write those numbers.
Have you got them all? How do you know?

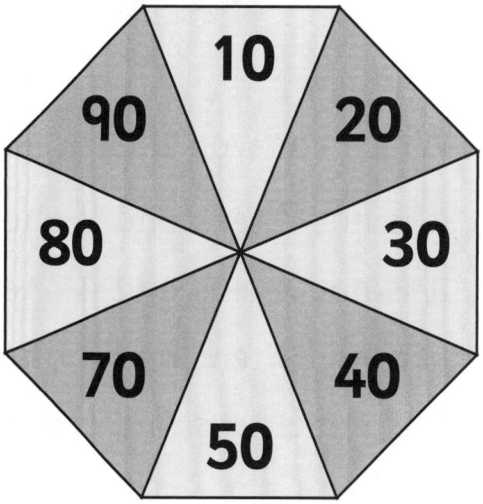

Hint: Use the place-value cards to make the numbers.
Use the 100 square to identify numbers that cannot be made.

Who won the race?

Remember
Two-digit numbers are made from tens and ones.

You will need:
resource 1, pages 52–3

Vocabulary
number pair, addition, total, digit, place-value cards, arrow cards

Which car won the race?

It is not 7 tens and 2 ones.
It is not 2 tens and 4 ones.
It is not 9 tens and 8 ones.
It is not 3 tens and 6 ones.

It is not 4 tens and 7 ones.
It is not 6 tens and 5 ones.
It is not 1 ten and 3 ones.
It is not 8 tens and 1 one.

Car number ☐ won the race.

Hint: Use place-value cards to make the two-digit numbers.

Unit 1A Number and problem solving
CPM Framework 1Nn4, 1Nn6, 1Pt2; CPM Teacher's Resource 7.2

Oliver's numbers

You will need: tens sticks and ones cubes or other base 10 apparatus; resource 1, pages 52–3

Vocabulary
number pair, addition, total, digit, place-value cards, arrow cards

Oliver used some tens sticks and ones cubes to make some numbers.

Then he made the matching number with place-value cards.

Do the numbers match?

Change the picture or the number to make them match.

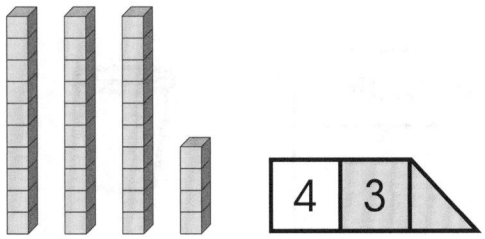

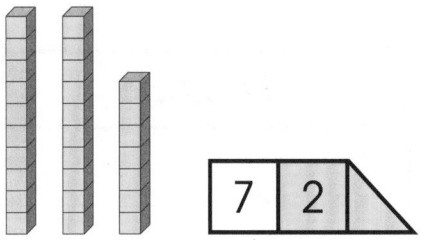

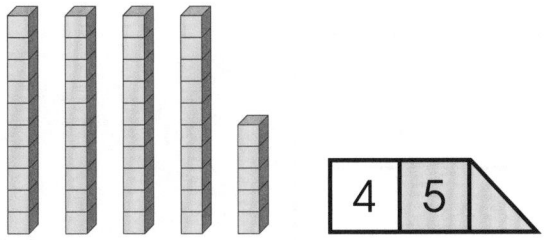

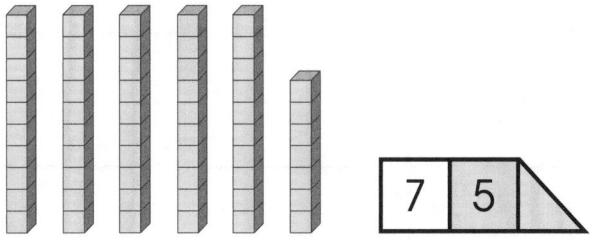

Which picture and number already matched? 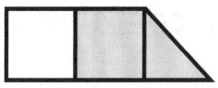

Hint: Use place-value cards to make the numbers shown by the tens sticks and ones cubes.

How many cupfuls?

Remember
When a container is empty, there is nothing in it. When a container is full, you cannot get any more in.

You will need: a litre jug, small bowl, saucepan and plastic bottle or similar items, plastic cup, counters, water, sand or rice to measure

Vocabulary
hold, compare, too much, same, estimate, most, least

Estimate how many cupfuls you will need to fill each container.

Now use a plastic cup to see if your estimate was close.

Record how many cupfuls you needed to fill each container.

Item	Estimate	Number of cupfuls

Tick the container that holds most.

Circle the container that holds least.

Hint: Remember to fill the cup to the top each time. Drop a counter into the container, with every cupful. Count the counters in each full container. The item that took the smallest number of cupfuls has the smallest capacity.

Balancing blocks

Remember
When the scales balance, both sides weigh the same.

You will need:
interlocking cubes, balance scales if any are available, or a coathanger with two plastic bags

Vocabulary
weigh, weighs, heavy, light, heavier, lighter, balance, same

Draw lines to join the shapes that you think will balance.

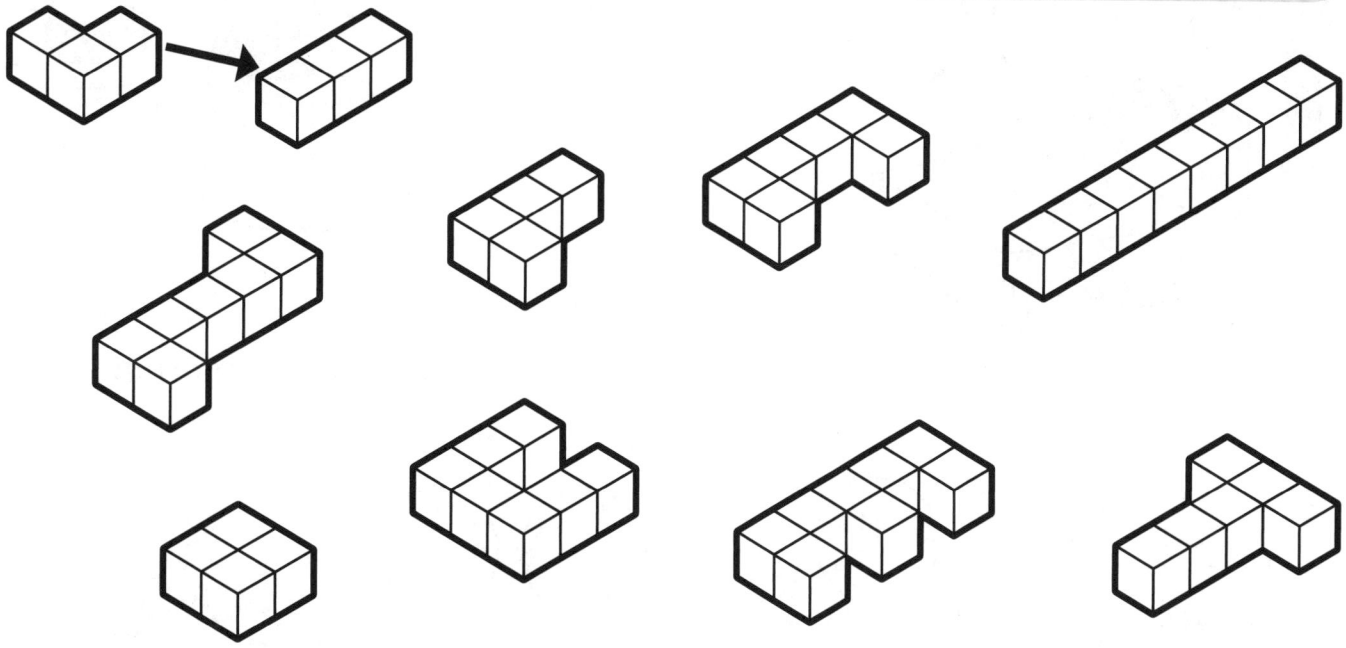

Check on a set of balance scales or a coathanger. If you need to make any changes, use a different coloured pencil.

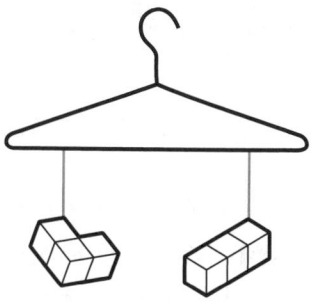

Hint: Count the cubes to find out if they will balance.

The correct time

Remember
The **minute hand** is the long hand. It points to the 12 for an o'clock time.
The **hour hand** is the short hand. It points to the hour number.

You will need: a clock with movable hands (You could make a clock from a paper plate, a split pin and two cardboard hands.)

Vocabulary
morning, afternoon, today, before, after, hour, o'clock, clock

Draw a ring around the clock that shows the correct time.

It is 7 o'clock in the morning.

It is 10 o'clock in the morning.

It is 3 o'clock in the afternoon.

It is 5 o'clock in the afternoon.

Hint: Move the hands on the clock to show the right time. Check which clock matches.

Travel times

You will need: a clock with movable hands

Vocabulary
hour, o'clock, clock

Remember
Count on from the first hour number to the second hour number to find the length of time.

How long did each journey take?

Example:

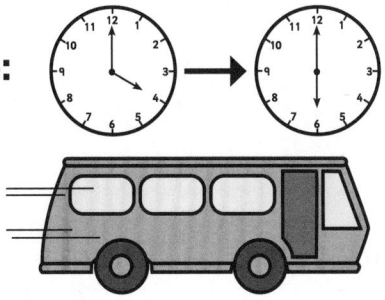

2 hours

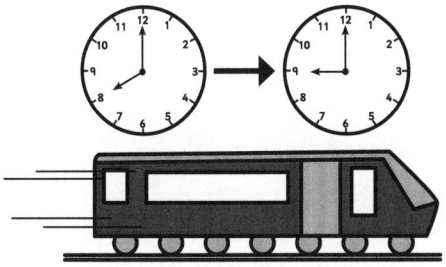

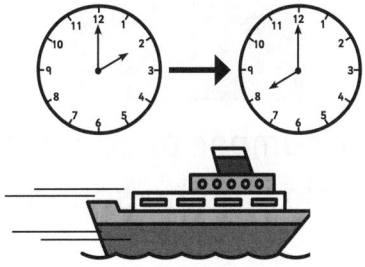

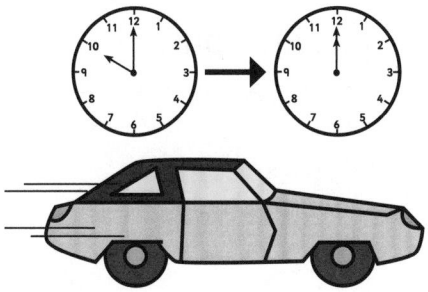

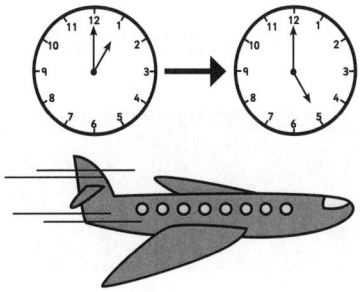

Hint: Set the clock to show the first time.
How many hours will it take to get to the second time?

Chocolate investigation

Remember
An even number can always be shared equally between two. An odd number is 1 more or less than an even number.

You will need:
cubes or counters

Vocabulary
odd, even, pair

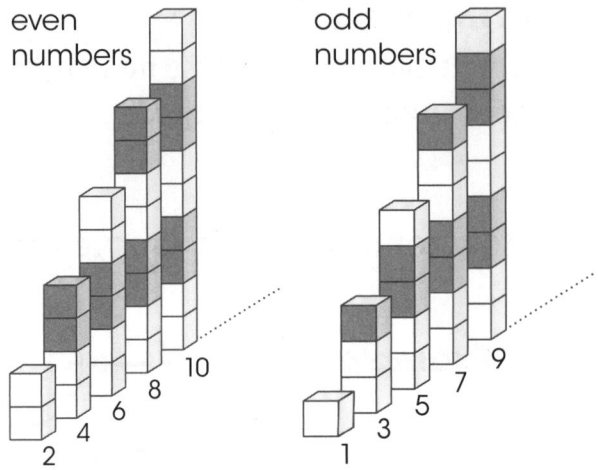

Mia and Finn have been given a bar of chocolate.

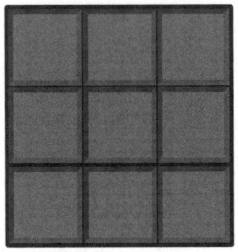

Mia got an even number of squares and Finn got an odd number. How many squares could they each have got?

Draw or write what you find out.

Another chocolate bar had 12 squares. This time, both children got an odd number of squares.

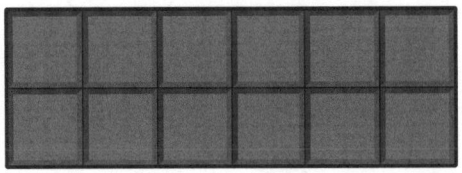

Draw or write what you find out.

Hint: Use cubes or counters to represent the squares of chocolate.

Unit 2A Number and problem solving
CPM Framework 1Nn5, 1Pt2; CPM Teacher's Resource 11.1, 11.2

Sharing sweets

You will need:
cubes or counters

Arman and Danna were given a bag of sweets.

When they shared them equally, there was one sweet left over.

Sarah, Vasu and David joined them, so they started again and shared the sweets equally.

This time there were two sweets left over.

If there were fewer than 20 sweets in the bag, how many sweets could there have been?

Draw or write what you find out.

There could have been ☐ or ☐ sweets in the bag.

Hint: Use cubes or counters to find out what happened.

Order

Remember
Ordinal numbers link order with counting numbers.

You will need:
a number line or resource 2, page 54

Vocabulary
ordering, ordinal, ones, first, 1st, second, 2nd, third, 3rd ...

Match the numbers with the words.

2nd → second

12th

fifth

5th

twelfth

9th

eighteenth

18th

fifteenth

15th

ninth

Hint: Use the number line to check the ordinal numbers.

Ordering numbers

You will need:
a number line or resource 2, page 54

Remember
When ordering numbers, look at the tens first, then the ones.

Vocabulary
tens, ones, less, more, order, smallest, greatest

Put the numbers in each list in order, from smallest to largest.

18, 15, 12, 16

27, 23, 17, 19

28, 34, 26, 31

41, 29, 37, 33

21, 43, 12, 34, 41, 14

Which numbers are between 17 and 20?

Which numbers are between 23 and 29?

Which numbers are between 19 and 22?

Which numbers are between 27 and 33?

Which numbers are between 38 and 42?

Hint: Use a number line or 100 square to order numbers and find **numbers between**.

Missing numbers

Remember
When you use a number line, jump to the right when adding.

You will need:
a number line or resource 2, page 54

Vocabulary
add, addition, altogether

Add the numbers together to find the missing numbers.

Add 5 and 2 to make 7

+	2	7
5	7	12
2	4	9

+	1	3
5		
7		

+	2	0
7		
9		

+	4	7
6		
8		

+	9	0
10		
9		

+	5	2
13		
15		

Hint: Draw the jumps on the number line to help find the totals.

Unit 2A Number and problem solving
CPM Framework 1Nn1, 1Nn2, 1Nc8; CPM Teacher's Resource 13.2, 13.5

Number paths

Remember
When you use a number line, jump to the right when adding and jump to the left when subtracting.

You will need:
a number line or resource 2, page 54

Vocabulary
subtraction, subtract, take away, less, difference, amount

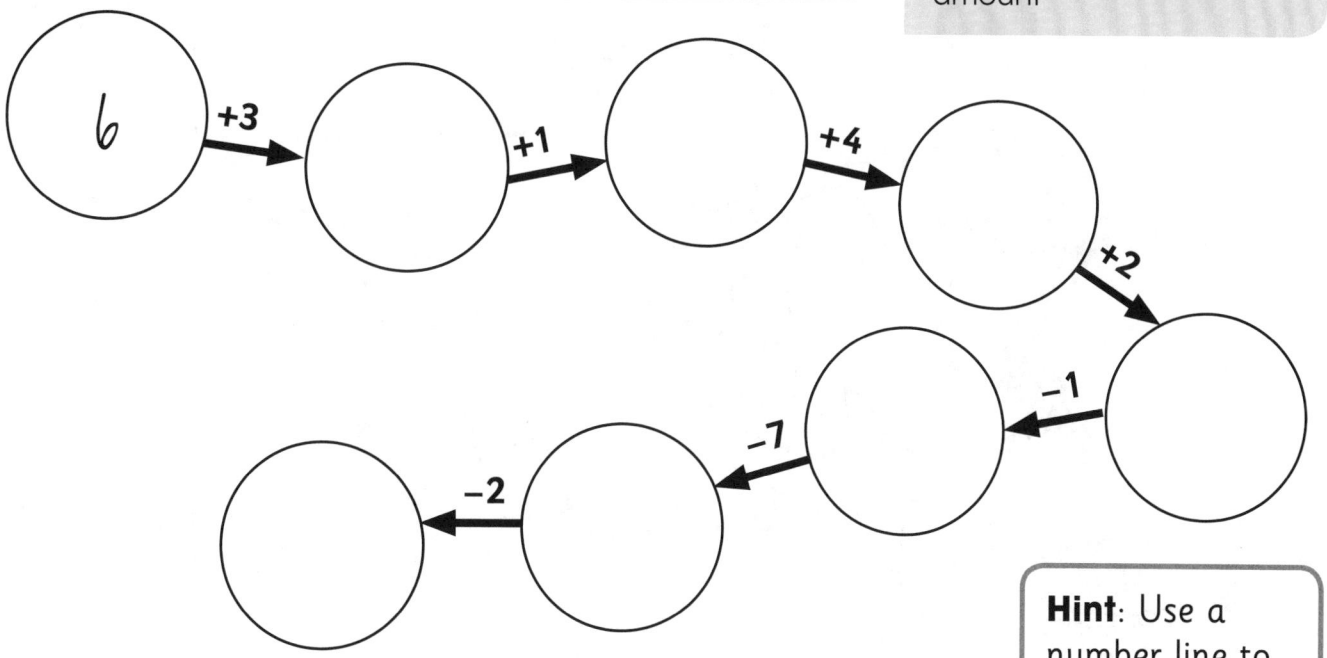

Hint: Use a number line to keep track of the numbers along the path.

Start with the 6 in the first circle. Move along the path. Follow the direction of the arrows.

Fill in the circles. What happens?

_____

_____

Start with a different number. What happens?

_____

_____

Will this always happen? How do you know?

_____

_____

Difference track

Vocabulary
difference, subtract, subtraction, take away, less

You will need: two different coloured counters or coins, two dice, see resource 3, page 55

This is a game for two players.

Take turns to throw two dice.

Find the difference between the two numbers.

Move on that number of spaces.

If you land on a shaded stone, miss your next turn.

Who gets home first?

Unit 2A Number and problem solving
CPM Framework 1Nn1, 1Nn2, 1Nc8, 1Nc9, 1Nc10, 1Nc11, 1Nc12; CPM Teacher's Resource 13.4, 13.5

Hint: Change the rules. For example, 'Land on an odd number, move on 1 space.'

Mr Pattern

Remember
Work systematically, changing one object at a time, to find all possibilities.

You will need:
resource 4, page 56, to plan the outfits

Vocabulary
combinations, systematic, possibilities

Mr Pattern likes to wear a different outfit each day. On Monday Mr Pattern wears a spotty hat, zig-zag T-shirt and spotty trousers. Draw the patterns to give him a different outfit each day.

Hint: Change only one item of clothing at a time.

Broken 100 square

Remember
Two-digit numbers are made from tens and ones.

You will need:
resource 2, page 54, to check against when finished

Each shape is part of the 100 square.

Write the missing numbers in each part of the 100 square.

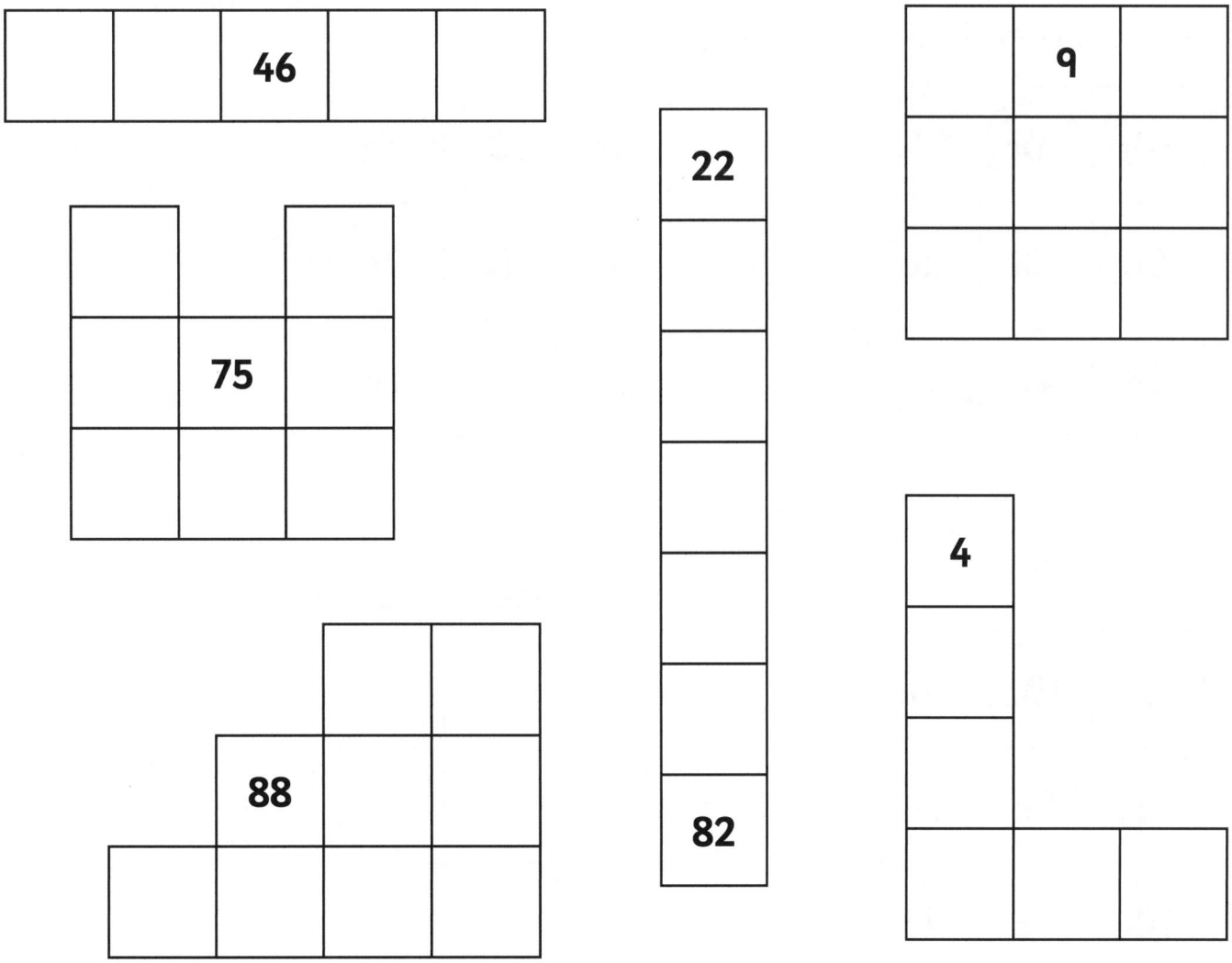

Hint: Count in ones along a row and in tens up or down a column.

Coin grids

Remember
You can use what you know about numbers to help you add money.

You will need: coins of all denominations of local currency or resource 5, page 57

Vocabulary
money, more, less, how much, total, count, coin, amount

Example

1c	1c	1c	3c
2c	5c	1c	8c
5c	10c	10c	25c
8c	16c	12c	

Add the coins in each row.
Add the coins in each column.

10c	10c	10c	____
5c	10c	2c	____
2c	2c	1c	____
____	____	____	

5c	10c	10c	____
5c	2c	2c	____
5c	5c	1c	____
____	____	____	

25c	10c	10c	____
25c	5c	2c	____
10c	1c	2c	____
____	____	____	

Now make up your own.

			____
			____
			____
____	____	____	

Hint: You can use dollars and cents or your local currency.

How tall?

You will need: cubes/squares, ideally 1 centimetre, or use strips from resource 6, page 58

Remember
When comparing length or height, line up objects edge to edge and from the same starting point.

Vocabulary
length, long, tall, short, longer than, compare

Use cubes to measure the height of each character.

cubes cubes cubes cubes

On a piece of paper, draw two more characters. Make one taller than the king, the other shorter than the rabbit.

How many cubes tall are your characters? ☐ and ☐

Hint: Start from the bottom of the character and place cubes along the full height.

Whose drinks?

Vocabulary
empty,
nearly empty,
nearly full, full,
least, less, more,
most

Remember
A nearly empty jug and a nearly full jug will make a full jug.

empty | nearly empty | nearly full | full

Match the boxes of drinks to the characters.

The kangaroo drinks the most.

The mouse drinks the least.

The king drinks more than the mouse but less than the girl.

The girl drinks less than the kangaroo.

A

B

C

D

E

Hint: Try putting jugs together.

Unit 2A Measure and problem solving
CPM Framework 1MI2, 1Pt2; CPM Teacher's Resource 17.1, 17.2

Days of the week

Vocabulary
day, week, Monday, Tuesday....

Remember
The days of the week are like numbers, they always come in the same order.

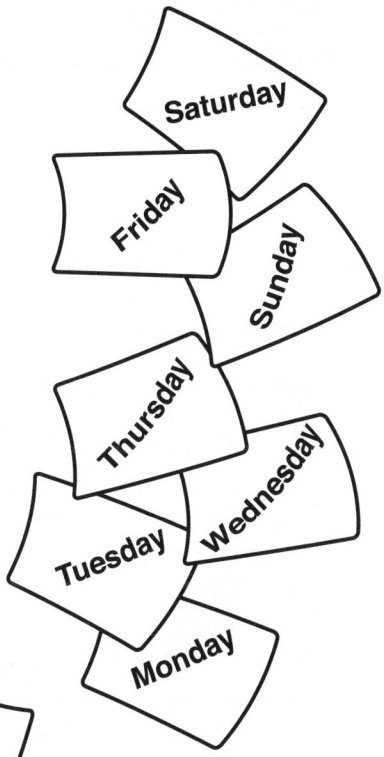

The day after Friday is _____.

The day before Tuesday is_____.

The day after Wednesday is _____.

The day before Sunday is _____.

Complete the table.

The day before	Today	The day after
	Thursday	
Sunday		
		Sunday
	Tuesday	

Hint: Say the days of the week in order to find the **day before** and the **day after**.

Going home

You will need:
a number line

Vocabulary
count, sort, group, set, same, different, block graph

Remember
Block graphs can be used to sort and group information. A **block graph** gives a picture of how many there are of something.

Look at the picture. How is each child travelling home?

Each column in the block graph shows one form of transport.
Colour half a square for each child using that form of transport.
One cyclist has been done for you.

Unit 2B Handling data and problem solving
CPM Framework 1Nn2, 1Nn3, 1Nn5, 1Dh1, IPt2; CPM Teacher's Resource 19.1, 19.2

Hint: Cross out the children as you add them to the graph.
Use a number line to count in twos.

Complete the block graph.

1 square = 2 children.

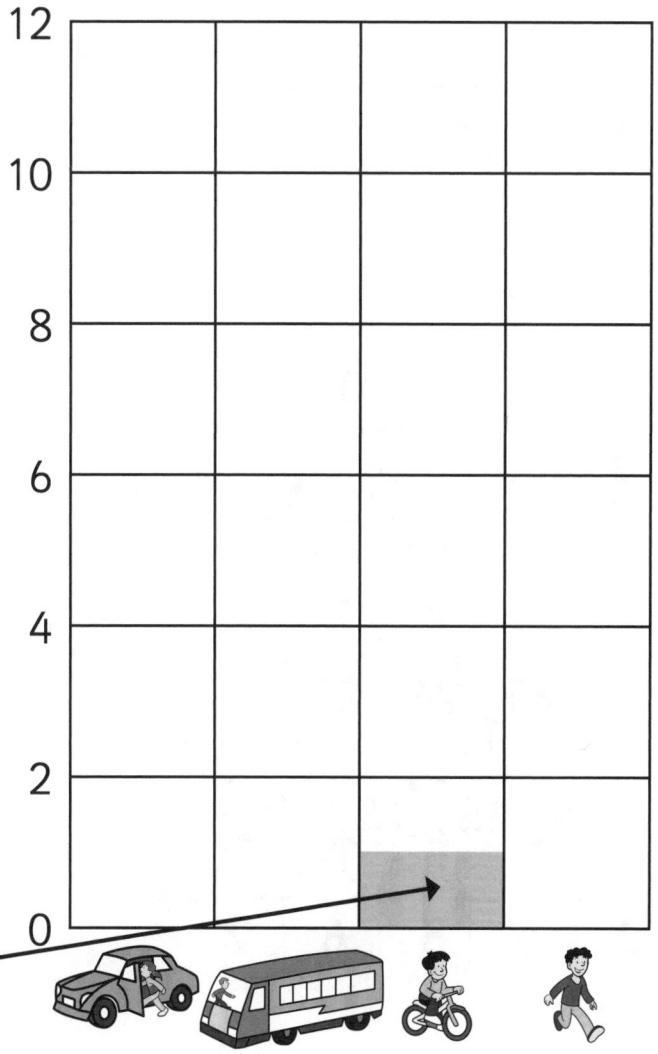

How many children altogether? ☐

Pyramid tens and ones

Remember
Adding 1 gives you the next counting number. Taking away 1 gives you the counting number before. When you add or subtract 10, the ones digit does not change.

Vocabulary
tens, ones, digit, number, place value, partition, more, less, add, subtract

Complete the pyramids as you follow the arrows.

Find the number at the top of the pyramid.

→ count on 1
↑ count on 10

Example:

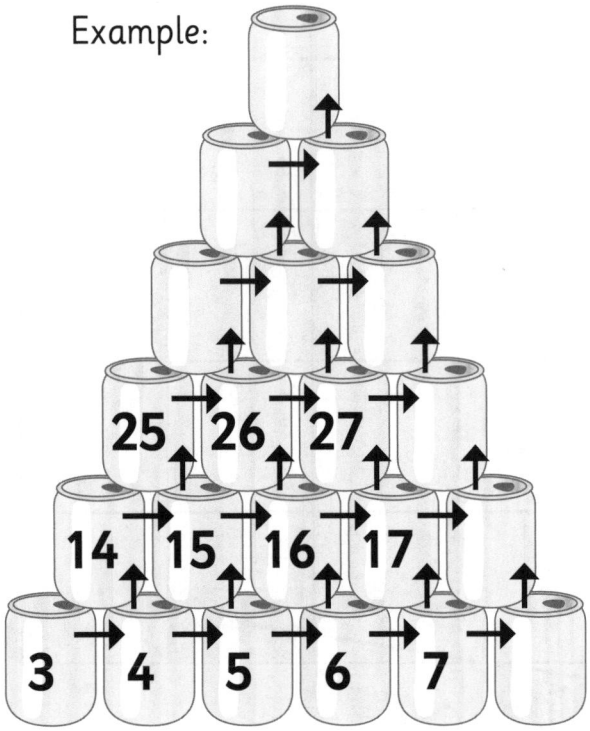

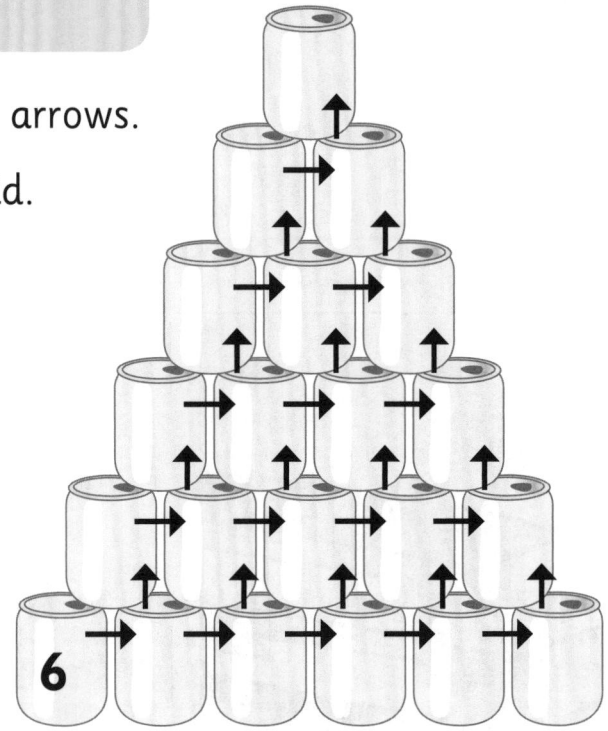

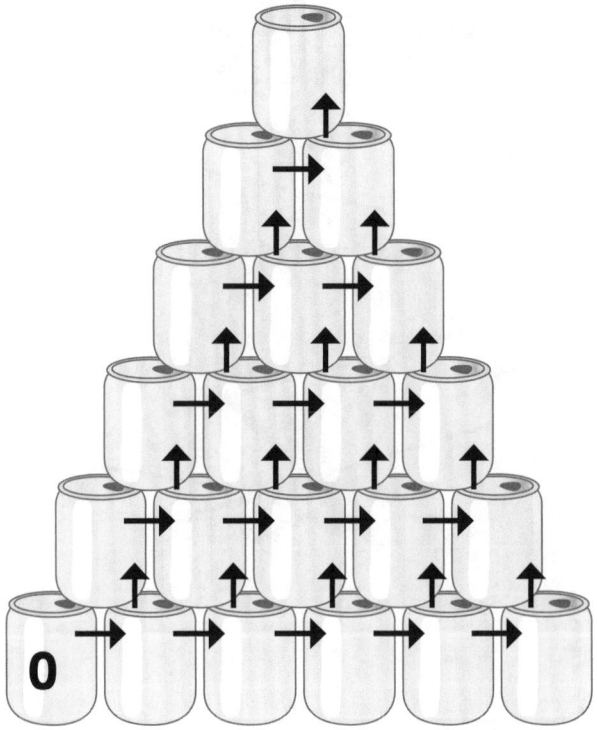

Hint: If necessary, use the 100 square to support counting on or back in tens or ones.

This time the number is already at the top of the pyramid.
What numbers will you write in the bottom row?

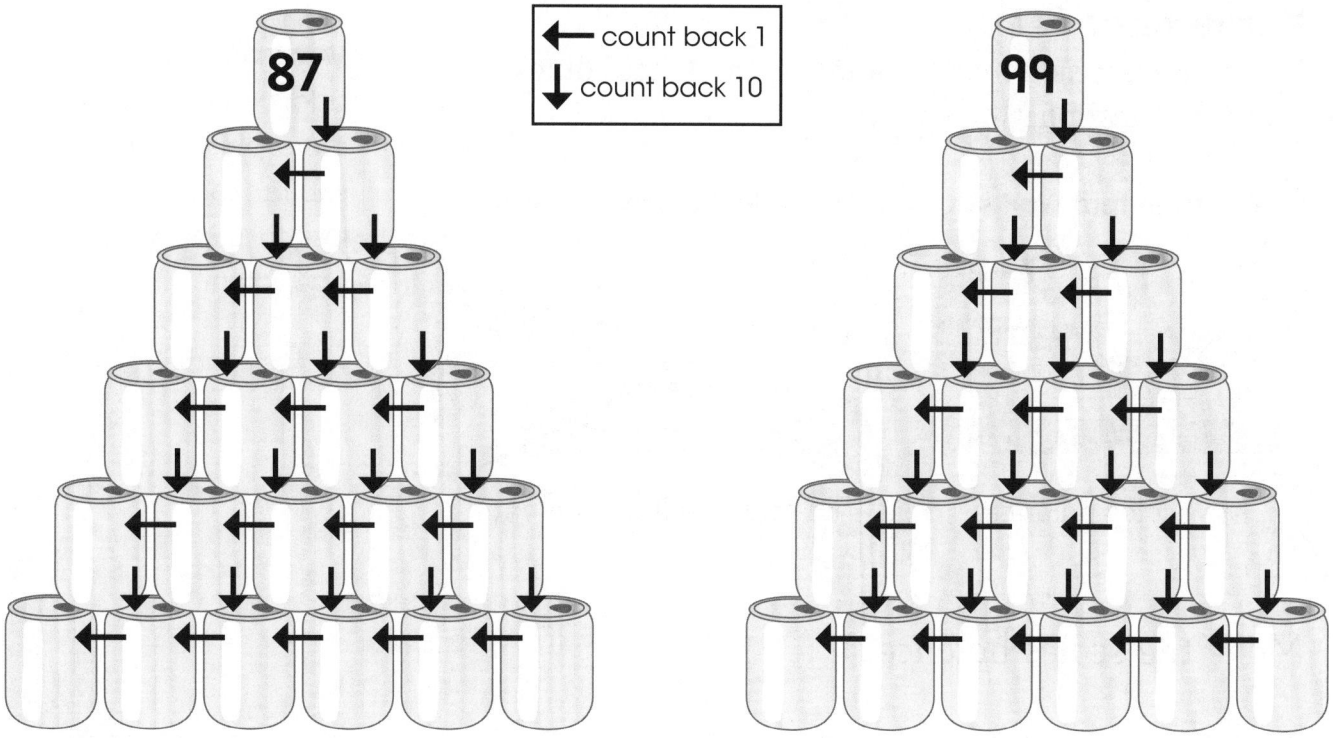

Now choose your own number to put in the top of each pyramid.
Then fill in the rest of the cans.

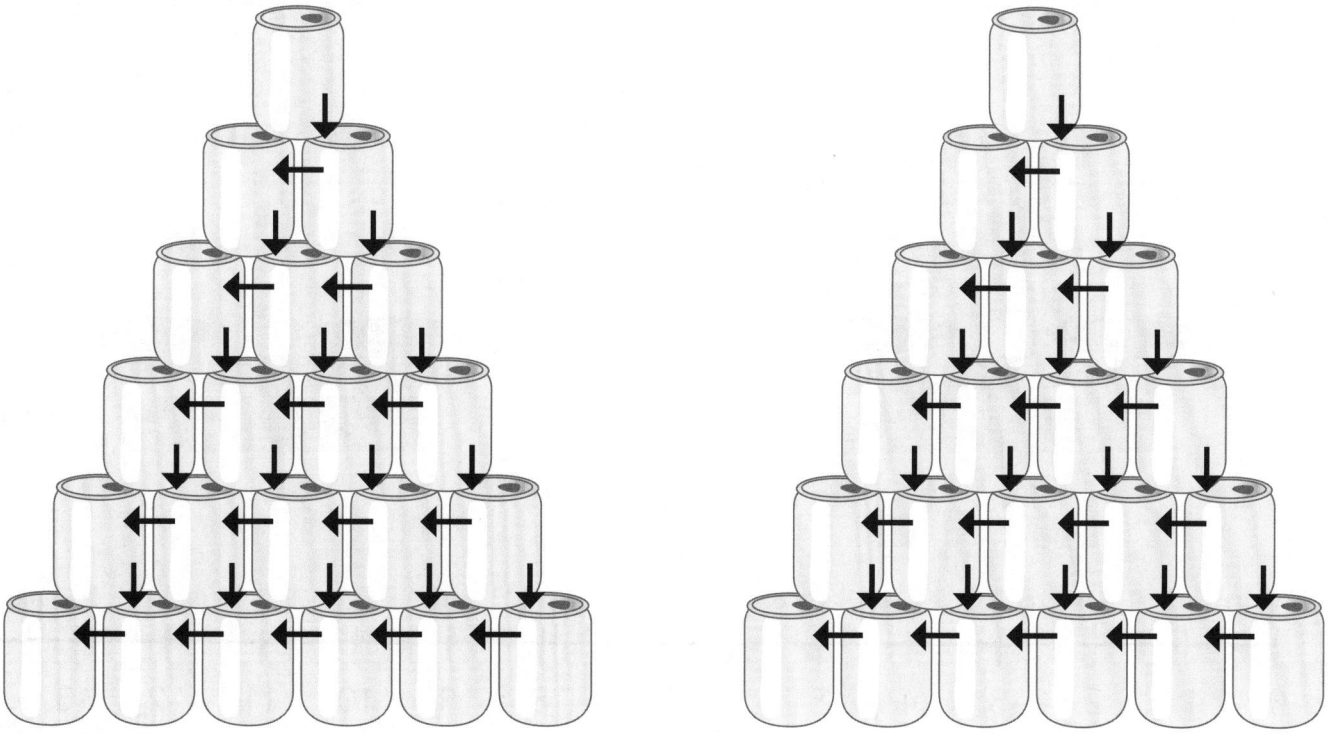

Balancing scales

Remember

For a number sentence to balance, the total values on both sides must be equal.

Example that works

6 + 3 **7 + 2**

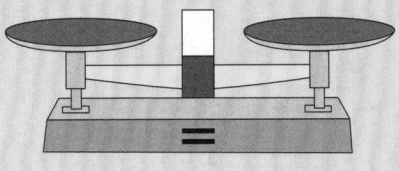

The scales balance

Example that doesn't work

6 + 3 **7 + 4**

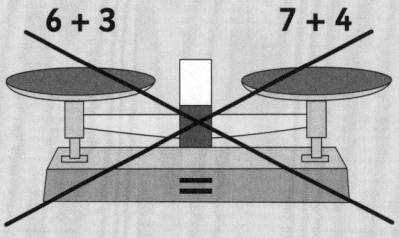

The scales will not balance

Vocabulary

add, combine, addition, more, plus, subtract, subtraction, minus, less, take away, equal, equivalent

Make the scales balance.

12 + 7 **+**

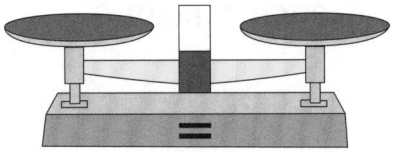

20 + 0 **+**

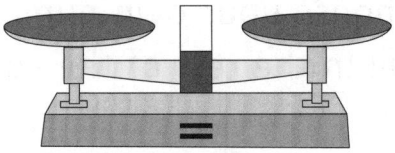

+ **+**

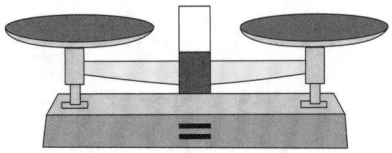

+ **14 – 7**

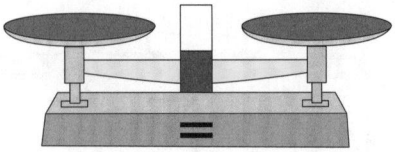

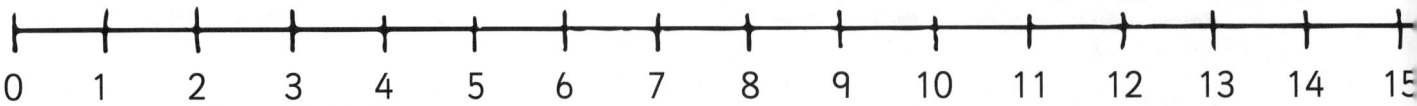

Unit 3A Number and problem solving
CPM Framework 1Nc8, 1Nc9, 1Nc11, 1Nc14, 1Nc18, 1Pt1; CPM Teacher's Resource 21.4

Make the scales balance.

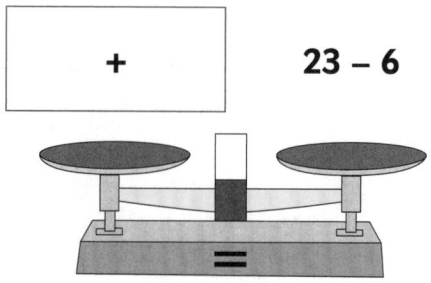

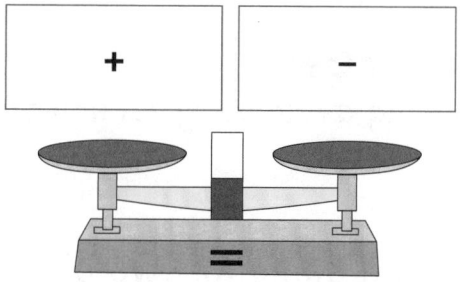

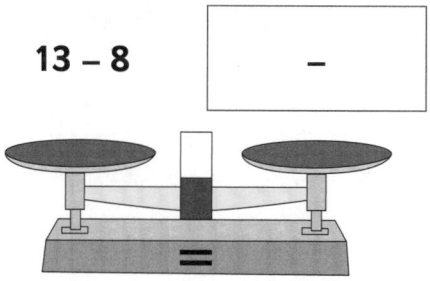

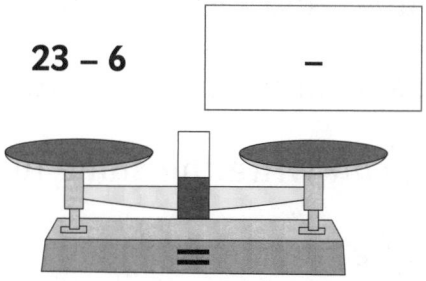

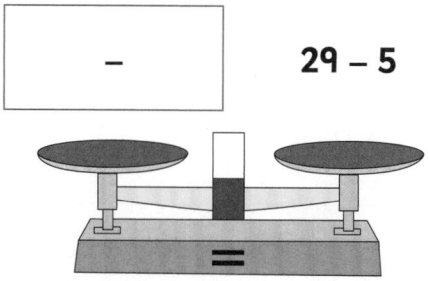

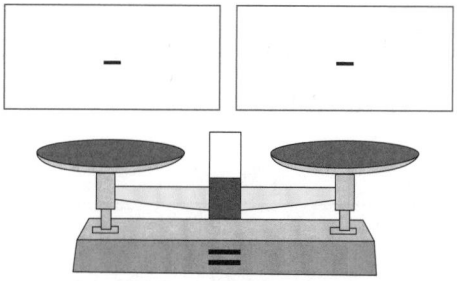

Hint: Use the number line to help you find an addition or subtraction calculation to make the scales balance.

Troubles with doubles

Remember
Doubling a number gives you twice as much.

You will need:
resource 7, page 59

Vocabulary
double

This is a game for two players.

Shuffle the number cards from the resource sheet.

Take turns to turn over the top card, double the number and write the answer in your grid.

Repeat until both grids are full.

You can write the same number more than once.

Shuffle the cards again.

Take turns to turn over a card, double the number and cross the answer off your grid. If the number is not on your grid, miss that turn.

The first player to cross off all the numbers on their grid wins.

Player 1		

Player 2		

Double or half

Remember
Halving gives you two equal amounts.

You will need: counters, a dice or resource 3, page 55

Vocabulary
double, half, whole, share, fair, equally

This is a game for two players.

1	2	3	4	5	6	7	8	9	10
11	12	13	14	15	16	17	18	19	20
21	22	23	24	25	26	27	28	29	30
31	32	33	34	35	36	37	38	39	40
41	42	43	44	45	46	47	48	49	50
51	52	53	54	55	56	57	58	59	60
61	62	63	64	65	66	67	68	69	70
71	72	73	74	75	76	77	78	79	80
81	82	83	84	85	86	87	88	89	90
91	92	93	94	95	96	97	98	99	100

Choose a target number.
This is the target for both players.
Players take turns to roll the dice.
Choose whether to double or halve the number.
Move the counter on by that many spaces.
The player who reaches the agreed target first wins.

Hint: Choose a smaller target number for a shorter game. Odd numbers can only be doubled.

Checking subtraction

Remember
A subtraction number sentence has two inverse number sentences, for example, 9 – 6 = 3 has inverse 6 + 3 = 9 and 3 + 6 = 9.

You will need:
a number line or resource 2, page 54

Vocabulary
add, adding, addition, total, subtract, inverse, number sentence

Draw a line to join each subtraction to the addition you would use to check it.

For the last two, complete the checking sentence.

9 – 6	6 – 9
	9 + 6
	6 + 3
11 – 7	7 + 4
	7 – 11
	7 + 11
14 – 9	9 – 14
	14 + 9
	9 + 5
21 – 7	14 + 7
	21 + 7
	7 – 21
24 – 8	24 + 8
	16 + 8
	8 – 24

15 – 9	6 + 9
	15 + 9
	9 – 15
13 – 6	6 – 13
	13 + 6
	7 + 6
26 – 9	17 + 9
	26 + 9
	9 – 26
29 – 6	6 + ☐
23 – 9	9 + ☐

Hint: Find the solution to the number sentence first, then think how to check that the solution is correct.

Balloon addition

Remember
You can use number pairs for 10 to make near tens.

You will need:
resource 8, page 60

Vocabulary
near, add, adding, addition, total, number sentence, number bond, number pair

Use the number bonds for 10 and near bonds for 10 to add the numbers in each set of balloons.

Example

10 + 1 + 10 + 1 = 22

_____

_____

_____

_____

_____

Hint: Pair the numbers into bonds for 10 or near bonds for 10.

Purses

Remember
Adding money is the same as adding numbers.

You will need:
a number line or resource 2, page 54, coins in local currency or resource 5, page 57, a paperclip and pencil to use the spinner

Vocabulary
money, coin, cent (or names of local currency), total

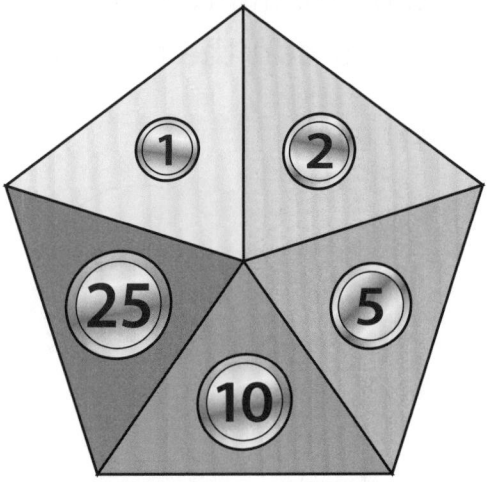

This is a game for two players.
The spinner tells you which coin to take.
Take turns to spin the spinner.
Place the coins on the matching coin purse.
Continue until one player has money in all five purses. The player with more money wins.

	Player 1		Player 2
1c		1c	
2c		2c	
5c		5c	
10c		10c	
25c		25c	

Unit 3C Measure and problem solving
CPM Framework 1Nc3, 1Nc8, 1Nc18, 1Mm1, 1Pt1, 1Pt2; CPM Teacher's Resource 24.1

Same lengths

Remember
To compare lengths, make sure that both objects start at the same place.

You will need: sticks of 2 cubes in one colour, sticks of 3 cubes in another colour, or resource 6, page 58

Vocabulary
long, short, just over, just under, about, longer than, shorter than

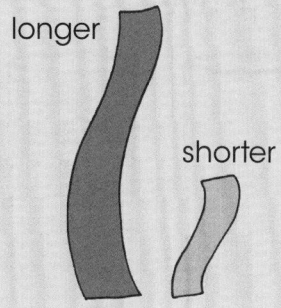

This is an activity for two people.

Player 1 has sticks of 3 cubes. Player 2 has sticks of 2 cubes.

Player 1 starts with one stick. Player 2 tries to make a stick of the same length.

Player 1 adds another stick to make a longer stick. Player 2 tries to make a stick of the same length.

Continue and complete the table.

Player 1 (3s)	**Player 2 (2s)**
Number of 3-sticks	Number of 2-sticks
1	Can't match
2	
3	
4	
5	
6	

What patterns can you see in the numbers in the table?

Alternatively, cut paper strips from resource 6 into twos and threes, discarding any cubes left over.

Hint: Focus on comparing the lengths of the sticks after every turn.

Which glass is left over?

Remember
To compare capacities, look at the size of each container and how much is in it.

Vocabulary
full, half full, empty, half empty, tall, short, compare, container, capacity, holds more, holds less

Read the clues below. Draw a line from each glass to its correct position to find which glass is left over.

1st	2nd	3rd	4th	5th	6th	7th

Clues:

The 3rd and 5th glasses are empty.

The 7th glass is tall and full of juice.

There is juice in the 2nd and 6th glasses.

The 1st glass is half full of water.

The 4th glass is tall and full of water.

The 5th and 6th glasses are short.

Draw the glass that is left over.

Draw and label the glass that is left over.

Hint: Before starting this activity, talk about the pictures. Use the suggested vocabulary to describe and compare the glasses.

Unit 3C Measure and problem solving
CPM Framework 1Nn9, 1Ml2, 1Pt2; CPM Teacher's Resource 26.2

Earlier and later

Remember
When working out a time that is an hour or hours later (or earlier) calculate just as you would with numbers.

You will need: a clock with movable hands (You could make a clock from a paper plate, a split pin and two cardboard hands.)

Vocabulary
clock, hands, hour, o'clock, earlier, later, morning, afternoon

Write the missing times in the grid.

2 hours earlier	Now	3 hours later
1 o'clock		
		11 o'clock

Draw a line from each clock to the new time, below.

4 hours earlier	6 hours later	5 hours earlier	3 hours earlier	5 hours later

Hint: Set the hands on the clock to the given time. Use the clock to help you find the new time.

Sorting toys

Remember
In order to represent data accurately, work systematically and make sure that you include all the information.

Vocabulary
count, fewer, sort, group, set, same, different, Carroll diagram

Sort the toys into two sets: those with wheels and those without wheels.

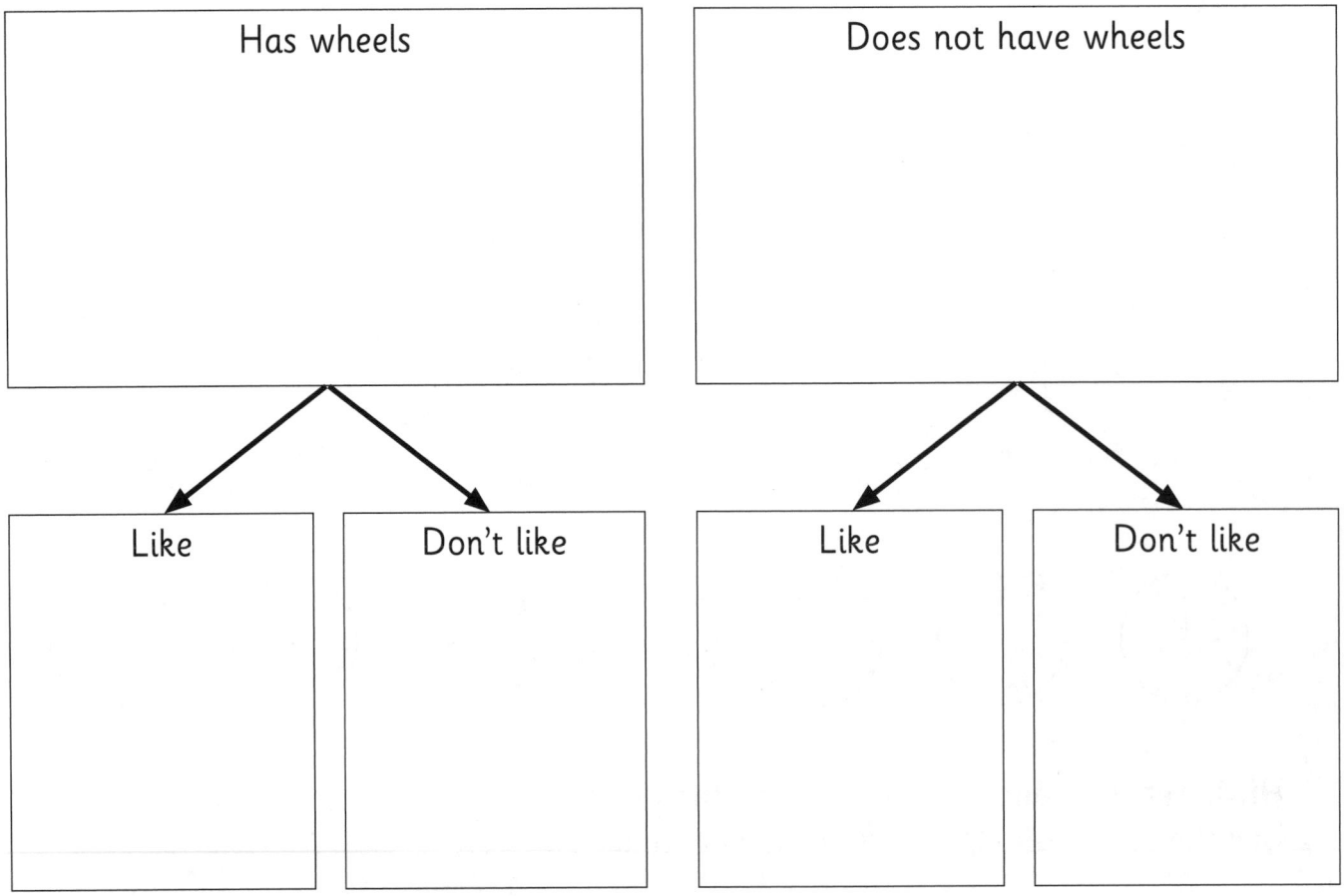

Now you are ready to put the toys into the Carroll diagram.

	Like	**Don't like**
Has wheels		
Does not have wheels		

Use the words **fewer**, **more** or **less** to complete the sentences.

I like toys with wheels _____ than toys without wheels.

There are_____ toys with wheels than without wheels.

Compare your results with someone else's. How are they are the same? How are they different?

_____

Resource 1 Place-value cards

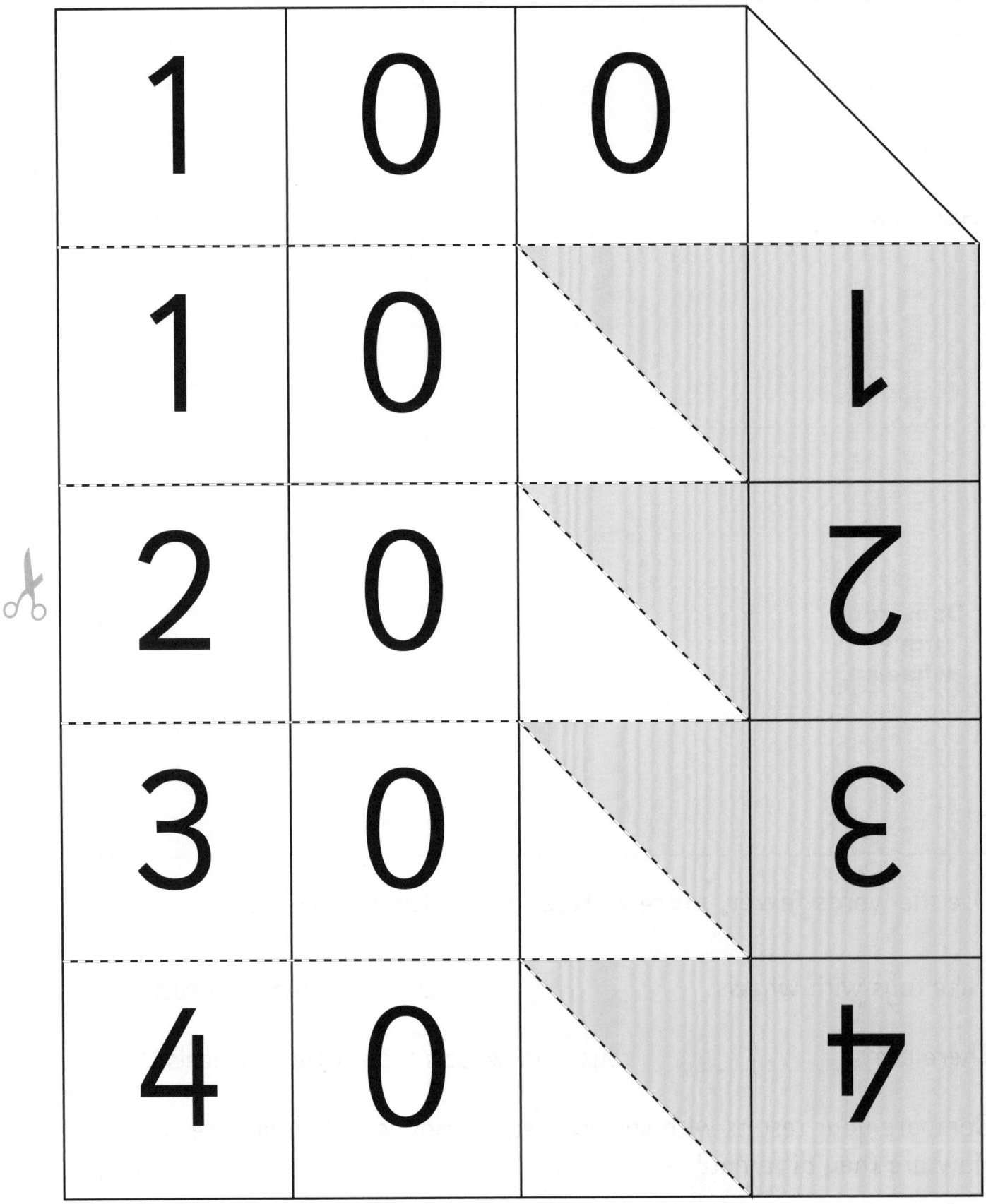

Original material © Cambridge University Press 2016

5	0		5
6	0		9
7	0		7
8	0		8
9	0		6

Original material © Cambridge University Press 2016

100 square

1	2	3	4	5	6	7	8	9	10
11	12	13	14	15	16	17	18	19	20
21	22	23	24	25	26	27	28	29	30
31	32	33	34	35	36	37	38	39	40
41	42	43	44	45	46	47	48	49	50
51	52	53	54	55	56	57	58	59	60
61	62	63	64	65	66	67	68	69	70
71	72	73	74	75	76	77	78	79	80
81	82	83	84	85	86	87	88	89	90
91	92	93	94	95	96	97	98	99	100

Original material © Cambridge University Press 2016

Resource 3 Dice template

Cut out the net, taking care not to cut off the tabs.
Fold along all the lines to make a cube.
Tuck the tabs inside and glue them in place, to hold the cube together.

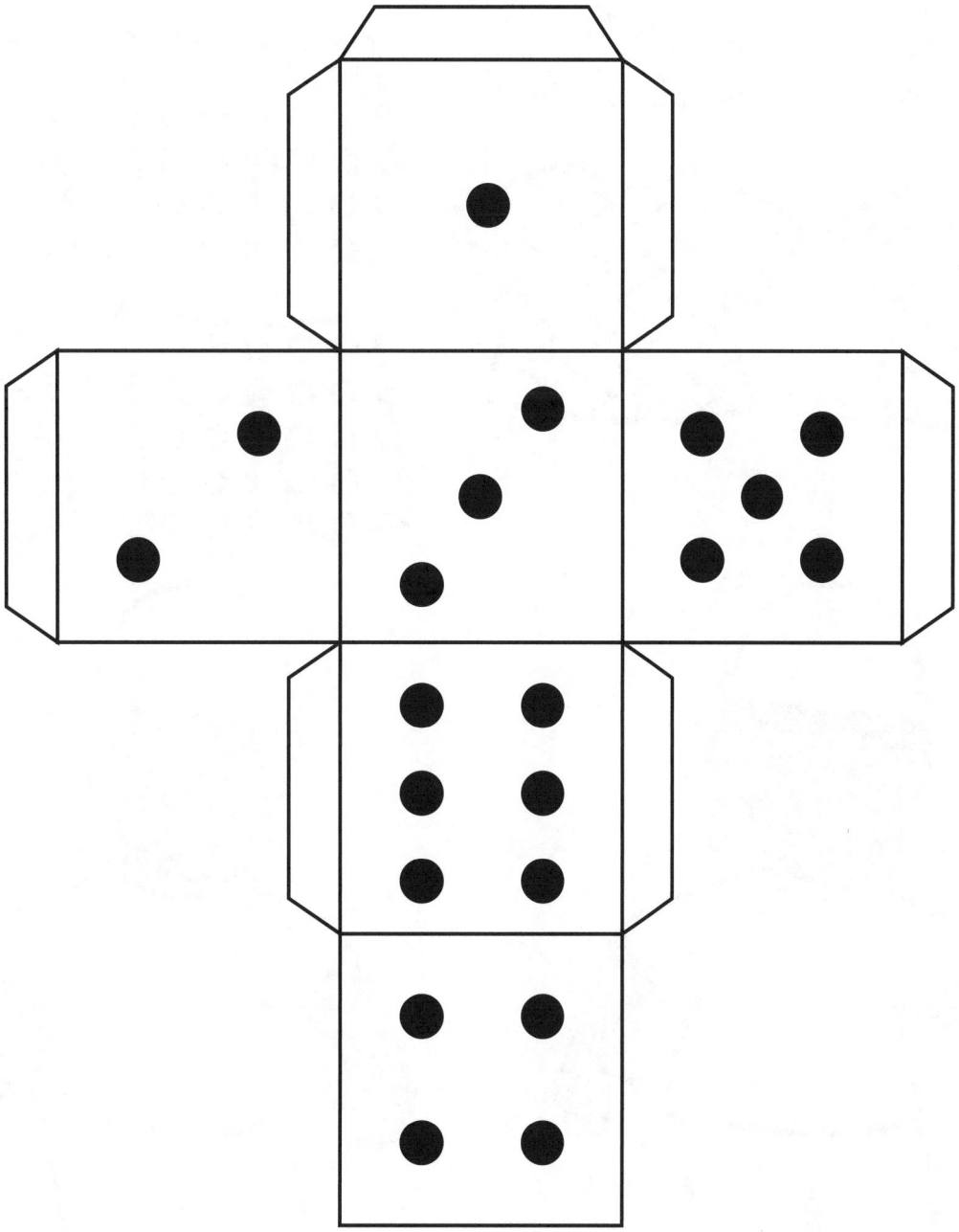

Original material © Cambridge University Press 2016

Resource 4
Mr Pattern

Original material © Cambridge University Press 2016

Resource 5 Coins

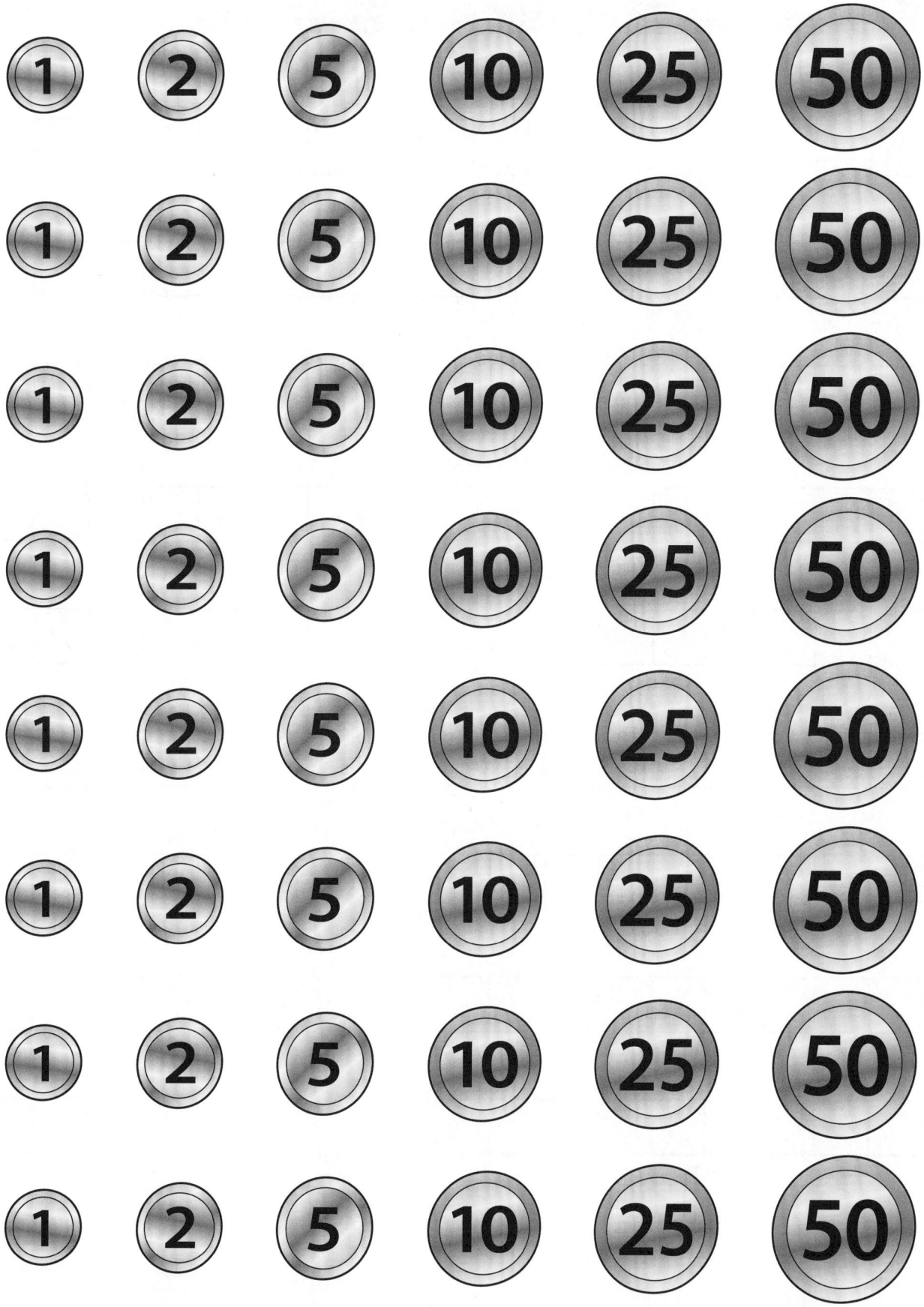

Original material © Cambridge University Press 2016

Resource 6
Centimetre squares

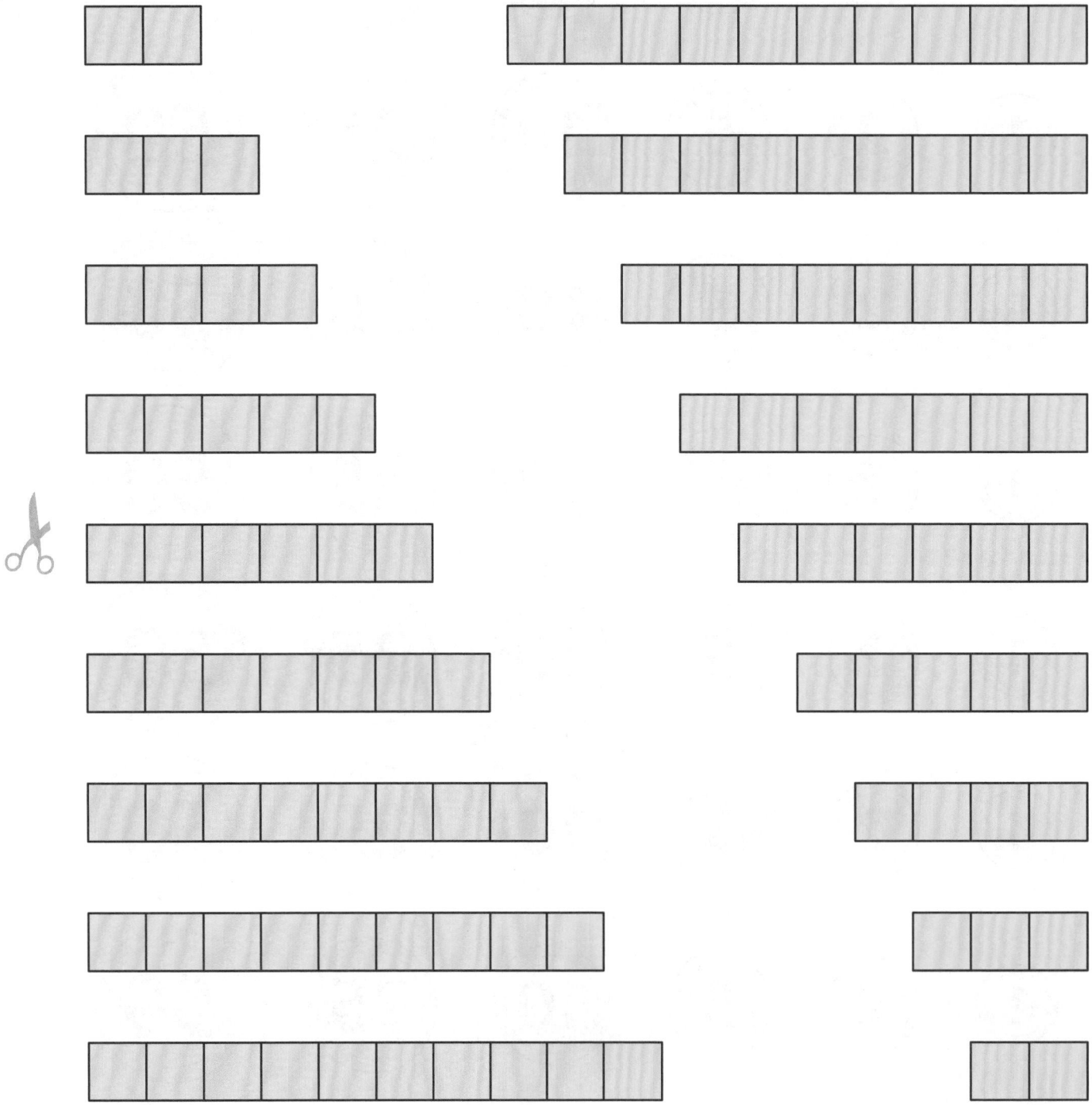

Original material © Cambridge University Press 2016

Resource 7 Digit cards 0 to 9

Cut the numbers from the resource and glue them onto thin card, for example, from a cereal box, so that you cannot see the number through the paper.

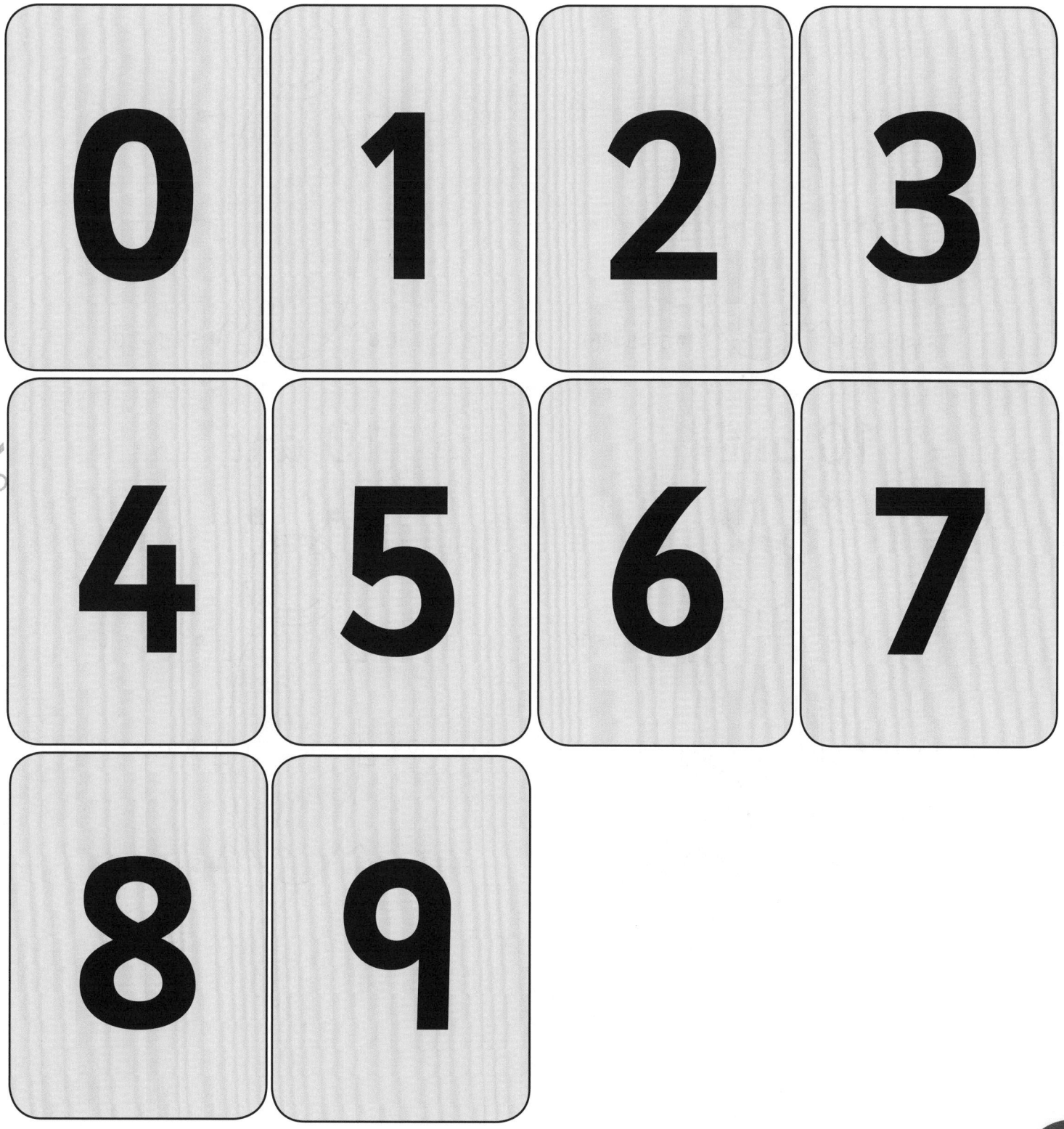

Original material © Cambridge University Press 2016

Resource 7 10 ant

10 ant

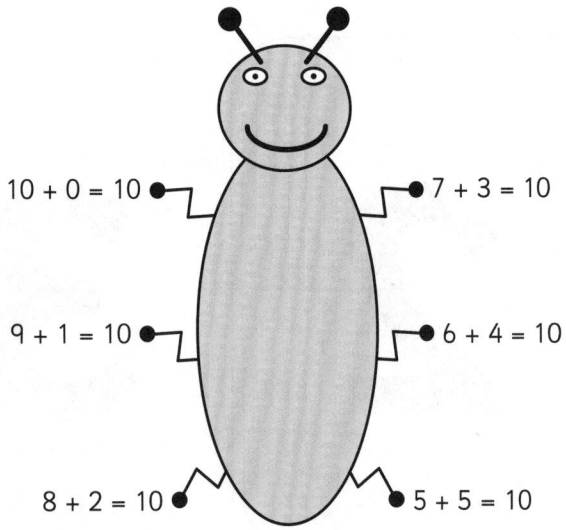

10 ant

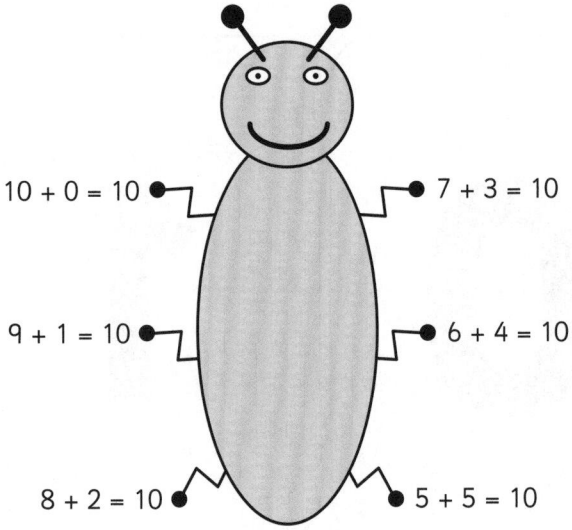

10 ant

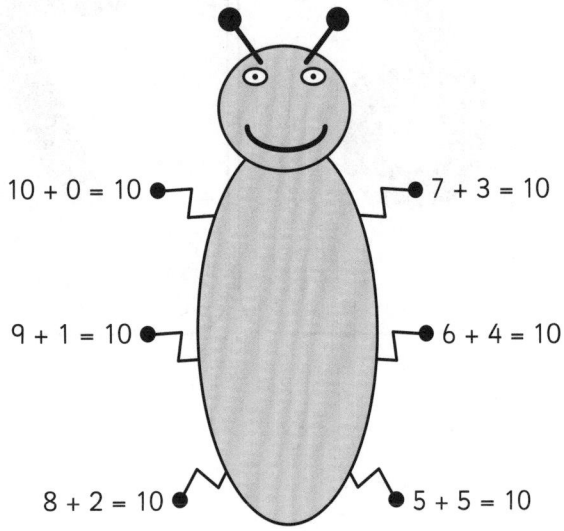

10 ant

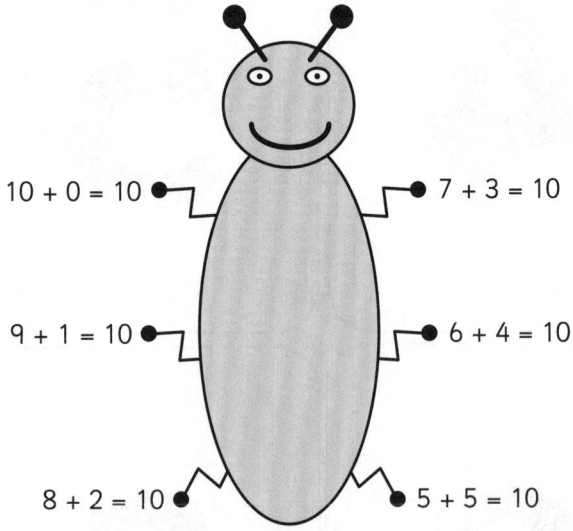

Original material © Cambridge University Press 2016

Answers

Page 4 Caterpillar numbers
The secret number is 7.

Page 5 Aeroplane numbers
The secret number is 3.

Page 6 Hands and feet
Children's own answers. Hand spans may be shorter than footprints, resulting in higher numbers when measuring with hand spans.

Page 7 Snakes
The shortest snake is 1 cube long (if 2 cm cubes are used).
The longest snake is 7 cubes long (if 2 cm cubes are used).
Other answers depend on the length of the child's pencil.

Page 8 Tens and ones
10 and 1 makes 11.
10 and 2 makes 12.
10 and 4 makes 14.
10 and 6 makes 16.
10 and 9 makes 19.
The lowest number I made is 11.
The highest number I made is 19.
Missing numbers: 13, 15, 17, 18.

Page 9 Numbers to 50

19 is 1 0 and 9
23 is 2 0 and 3
26 is 2 0 and 6
31 is 3 0 and 1
37 is 3 0 and 7
45 is 3 0 and 5
48 is 4 0 and 8

Children's own answers.

Page 10 My hand
Children's own answers.

Page 11 Number line numbers

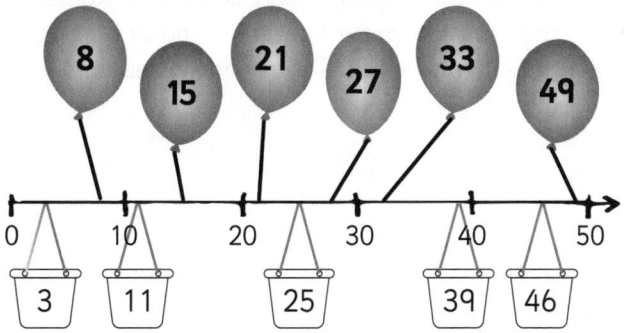

Page 12 2D shapes
10 triangles
12 circles
24 squares
15 rectangles.

Page 13 3D Shapes
1. cube, 2. pyramid, 3. cone, 4. cylinder.

Page 14 Symmetry

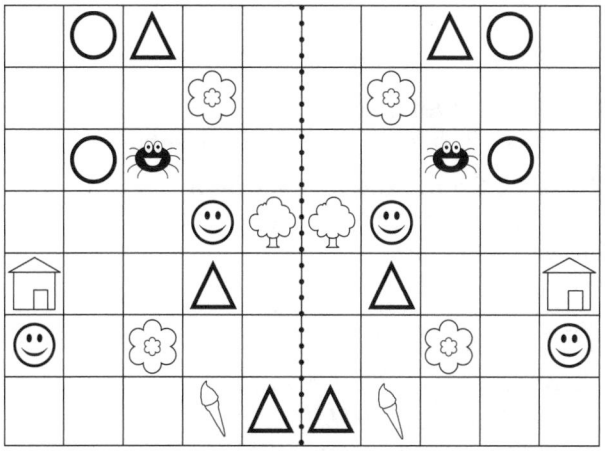

Page 15 Number spinners
Numbers 61 to 69 and 14, 24, 34, 44, 54, 74, 84 and 94 cannot be made because 60 and 4 are missing.

Page 16 Who won the race?
Car 59 won the race.

Page 17 Oliver's numbers
Answers will depend on whether the children decide to change the picture or the number.
1. 34 or 43; 2. 27 or 72; 3. 45; 4. 57 or 75.
Q3 is already matched.

Page 18 How many cupfuls?
Answers will depend on the containers and plastic cups used.

Page 19 Balancing blocks

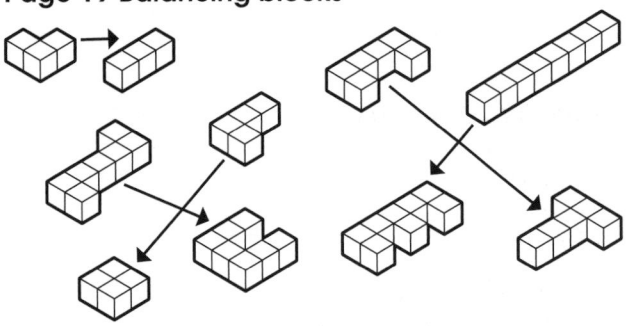

Page 20 The correct time

It is 7 a.m. It is 10 a.m.
It is 3 p.m. It is 5 p.m.

Page 21 Travel times

1. 1 hour; 2. 6 hours; 3. 2 hours; 4. 4 hours.

Page 22 Chocolate investigation

It is not expected that children will record their answers in a table.

9 squares:

Finn	Mia
1 square	8 squares
3 squares	6 squares
5 squares	4 squares
7 squares	2 square

12 squares:

Finn	Mia
1 square	11 squares
3 squares	9 squares
5 squares	7 squares
7 squares	5 squares
9 squares	3 squares
11 squares	1 square

Page 23 Sharing sweets

7 sweets (1 each) or 17 sweets (3 each).

Page 24 Order

Parrot 2nd → second
Elephant 12th → twelfth
Lion 5th → fifth
Monkey 9th → ninth
Giraffe 18th → eighteenth
Crocodile 15th → fifteenth

Page 25 Ordering numbers

12, 15, 16, 18
17, 19, 23, 27
26, 28, 31, 34
29, 33, 37, 41
12, 14, 21, 34, 41, 43
Which numbers are between 17 and 20?
18, 19.
Which numbers are between 23 and 29?
24, 25, 26, 27, 28.
Which numbers are between 19 and 22?
20, 21.
Which numbers are between 27 and 33?
28, 29, 30, 31, 32.
Which numbers are between 38 and 42?
39, 40, 41.

Page 26 Missing numbers

+	1	3
5	6	8
7	8	10

+	2	0
7	9	7
9	11	9

+	4	7
6	10	13
8	12	15

+	9	0
10	19	10
9	18	9

+	5	2
13	18	15
15	20	17

Page 27 Number paths

6, 9, 10, 14, 16, 15, 8, 6. Children's own answers. You will always finish on the same number as you started with because you are adding 10 then taking away 10.

Page 28–29 Difference track

Game – no answers.

Page 30 Mr Pattern

Mr Pattern dressed in:
Spotty hat with zig-zag T-shirt and zig-zag trousers.
Spotty hat with spotty T-shirt and spotty trousers.
Spotty hat with spotty T-shirt and zig-zag trousers.
Zig-zag hat with zig-zag T-shirt and zig-zag trousers.
Zig-zag hat with zig-zag T-shirt and spotty trousers.
Zig-zag hat with spotty T-shirt and spotty trousers.
Zig-zag hat with spotty T-shirt and zig-zag trousers.

Page 31 Broken 100 square

44	45	46	47	48

64		66
74	75	76
84	85	86

		79	80
	88	89	90
97	98	99	100

22
32
42
52
62
72
82

8	9	10
18	19	20
28	29	30

4		
14		
24		
34	35	36

Page 32 Coin grids

10c	10c	10c	30c
5c	10c	2c	17c
2c	2c	1c	5c
17c	22c	13c	

5c	10c	10c	25c
5c	2c	2c	9c
5c	5c	1c	11c
15c	17c	13c	

25c	10c	10c	45c
25c	5c	2c	32c
10c	1c	2c	13c
60c	16c	14c	

Children's own grid.

Page 33 How tall?

Using 1 cm cubes or squares:
Girl: 6 cubes or squares.
Mouse: 4 cubes or squares.
Rabbit: 10 cubes or squares.
King: 16 cubes or squares.

Page 34 Whose drinks?

King drinks set A.
Mouse drinks set D.
Girl drinks set B.
Rabbit drinks set E.
Kangaroo drinks set C.

Page 35 Days of the week

The day after Friday is Saturday.
The day before Tuesday is Monday.
The day after Wednesday is Thursday.
The day before Sunday is Saturday.

Complete the table.

The day before	Today	The day after
Wednesday	Thursday	Friday
Sunday	Monday	Tuesday
Friday	Saturday	Sunday
Monday	Tuesday	Wednesday

Pages 36–37 Going home

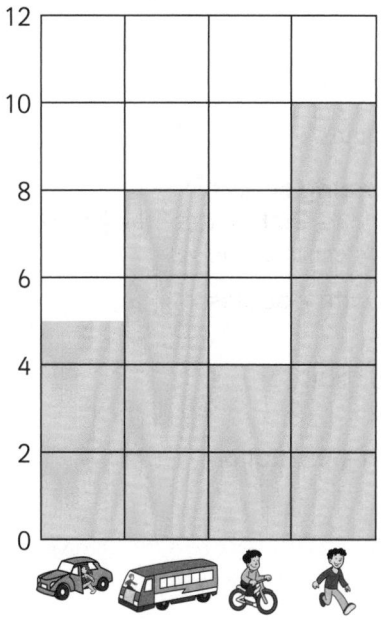

How many children altogether? 27.

Pages 38–39 Pyramid tens and ones

Completed pyramids:

58
47 48
36 37 38
25 26 27 28
14 15 16 17 18
3 4 5 6 7 8

61
50 51
39 40 41
28 29 30 31
17 18 19 20 21
6 7 8 9 10 11

55
44 45
33 34 35
22 23 24 25
11 12 13 14 15
0 1 2 3 4 5

87
76 77
65 66 67
54 55 56 57
43 44 45 46 47
32 33 34 35 36 37

99
89 90
77 78 79
66 67 68 69
55 56 57 58 59
44 45 46 47 48 49

Children's own pyramids.

Pages 40–41 Balancing scales
Children's own solutions. Both sides of the balance scales must be equivalent in value.

Page 42 Troubles with doubles
Game – no answers.

Page 43 Double or half
Game – no answers.

Page 44 Checking subtraction

9 – 6 ⟶ 6 + 3.
11 – 7 ⟶ 7 + 4
14 – 9 ⟶ 9 + 5
21 – 7 ⟶ 14 + 7
24 – 8 ⟶ 16 + 8
15 – 9 ⟶ 6 + 9
13 – 6 ⟶ 7 + 6
26 – 9 ⟶ 17 + 9
29 – 6 ⟶ 6 + **23**
23 – 9 ⟶ 9 + **14**

Page 45 Balloon addition
Set 2: 6 + 5 + 9 + 2
10 + 1 + 10 + 1 = 22
Set 3: 1 + 6 + 3 + 9
10 + 9 = 19 or 9 + 10 = 19
Set 4: 7 + 4 + 0 + 9
10 + 1 + 9 = 20
Set 5: 8 + 5 + 4 + 1
8 + 10 = 18 or 9 + 9 = 18
Set 6: 8 + 3 + 5 + 6
10 + 1 + 10 + 1 = 22

Page 46 Purses
Game – no answers.

Page 47 Same lengths
3 twos is the same length as 2 threes.
6 twos is the same length as 4 threes.
9 twos is the same length as 6 threes.
12 twos is the same length as 8 threes, and so on.
Each new matching length is reached when another 3 twos and 2 threes have been added.

Page 48 Which glass is left over?

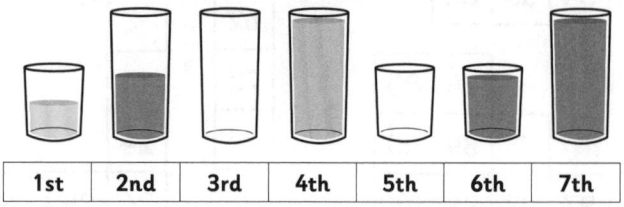

6th rule – 5th and 6th glasses are short, therefore there are no swappable glasses.

Leftover glass is 

Page 49 Earlier and later

2 hours earlier	Now	3 hours later
2 o'clock		7 o'clock
7 o'clock		12 o'clock
1 o'clock	3 o'clock	6 o'clock
6 o'clock	8 o'clock	11 o'clock

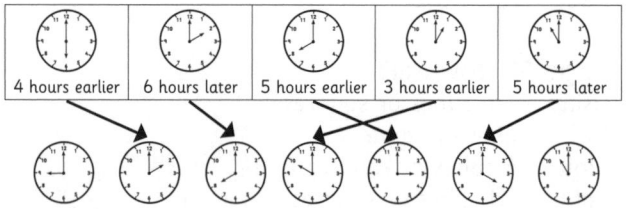

Pages 50–51 Sorting toys
Children's own answers.
There are fewer toys with wheels than without wheels.